Mastering The Music Business

Creative Empowerment: "It" Factor in the Music Industry

Written by Zaque Eyn

Text copyright © 2013, 2014 Zaque Eyn

All Rights Reserved

Table of Contents

Introduction..............Why Read This?, **4**
Chapter 1................End Game, **7**
Chapter 2................What is Success?, **11**
Chapter 3...............Entrepreneurship, **16**
Chapter 4................Goals and To-Do Lists, **18**
Chapter 5................Breaking Down Your Industry, **22**
Chapter 6................Do's and Don'ts of Listening, **27**
Chapter 7................Understanding The Company, **31**
Chapter 8................Persuasive Skills, **43**
Chapter 9................Writing Professionally, **51**
Chapter 10..............Professional Pitch, **64**
Chapter 11..............Professional Bio, **70**
Chapter 12..............Fact Sheet, **74**
Chapter 13..............Press Kit, **77**
Chapter 14..............Professional Life, **81**
Chapter 15..............Networking, **86**
Chapter 16..............Meetings, **92**
Chapter 17..............Industry Checklist, **95**
Chapter 18..............Selecting Your Team, **99**
Chapter 19..............Marketing, **106**
Chapter 20..............Branding, **127**
Chapter 21..............Putting it Together, **136**
Chapter 22..............The Future, **152**
Chapter 23..............Egos, **159**
Chapter 24..............Confidentiality Agreement, **167**
Chapter 25..............Empower Your Creativity, **170**

Introduction

I have always been a creative entrepreneur, and not allowed the world to get the better of me, but instead, let the world fuel me. Throughout 13 years in the music industry I've worked with some of the best in the business: Anita Baker, KC Porter, Jim Henson Studios, Michael Jackson (Never Land), OK GO, George Duke, Lauren Mayhew, Pomplamoose, and as far as I can remember, I've heard of "it," this elusive thing setting apart the extraordinary from the ordinary. These people encapsulate: auras, energy, and empower all that are near; you're drawn to them.

I remember the first time I was pointed out amongst a group of peers as having "it." The moment raised my energy, raising the energy of everyone else around, in turn, raising my energy even more. I felt: invigorated, aware, and enlightened. All these sensations stemmed from a comment by the person running the show, we all looked up to, and wanted to be like. After the day was over, at home, having a chance to soak it all in, I realized I had arrived, and started wondering what "it" actually was. Can anyone learn to have and apply "it?"

Books and school seem an obvious choice, until you realize answering the question isn't simply a matter of reading and going to school, because real world experience, combined with a multitude of questions, is necessary.

One thing I never found, from books or school, was anything explaining what I needed in order too have the right game plan in place to strive towards greatness and beyond. I've read countless books, on a multitude of topics, in search of that elusive "it" factor; never truly finding what it was I needed to do to have "it." Nothing has ever broken "it" down.

In fact, not only has a book never gotten to the heart of "it," but school will never be able to teach what "it" is. It is an impossibility for a school to teach this, because "it" is something, I have learned, that comes from real world experiences combined with knowing how to apply techniques, rarely spoken about, and geared towards the music industry. It takes various topics to answer the "it" factor, and who has time to get four or five different degrees and learn how to apply them all?

Certainly I have learned from celebrities, school, and real world experiences about "it," and what it takes to have "it," while working with everyone. But every time someone says I have "it," and I ask what "it" is, they always give me a different answer than the person before. This got me thinking how much of a struggle the music industry is and how many books someone would need to buy and read, not to mention the years of school, in order to have the knowledge of implementing and understanding the "it" factor.

And it goes deeper than just reading 100 + books over the course of you're career, or start of. To this day I had yet to find anything going beyond the normal hoopla of "you need a marketing plan, or goals in place, EPK." Nothing ever had the real talk, the true marketing plan outline, the right way to network, and in all the same place. Sure I've read music industry books that have a marketing plan outline, but it's not a professional outline, one I could use to land real clients, they are simply geared at musicians who need an understanding of some basics. What is anyone to do if they want to write a real marketing plan for a record label? You'd most certainly need to go to school in order to do this. No one book on the market will ever teach you this, unless you know what school book to buy, and even then these books fail to give a real outline. What if someone needed to set up a meeting, set realistic goals, coach website logistics, build business rapport, understand egos or understand body language, and really make a living in the music industry?

These are questions we could spend a lifetime trying to answer by reading hundreds of books. Or we could go to school for 8 years and get a masters degree, but the reality is we'd still never get everything we needed because even the best of schools fail to teach us everything. If you go to school for a music degree, or music business degree, they don't teach you things like body language, let alone how to implement it in the music business, if you are lucky enough to even take the course.

This brings me to the reason for writing this book. I wanted to give everyone the opportunity to know what it really takes to survive in the music industry. An opportunity to learn the skills required, and offer professional tools, that can be applied to all aspects of the industry, not just a guitar player marketing plan that means nothing or can be applied to anything outside of a niche aspect. A true music industry book designed for all aspects; a book with skills to take a record label head on, manage a career, or give true A&R help. A book where one could start, or advance, they're career, and become successful.

Throughout this book you will learn the various techniques top professionals in the music industry apply in their careers. But you are not going to get something geared towards musicians only, you will be getting the knowledge to implement a successful career in any aspect of the industry: starting your business, career development, artist development, managing other people and so on. And as far as that elusive "it" factor, well, everything combined and implemented in this book will give you that "it" factor and empower your creativity, and career, for years to come.

Lastly, this book is not a simple read me and apply me book, it goes beyond the normal spectrum of other books because I have included classes of sorts for everyone reading it. At the end of this book you will find a section to continue your education and truly help take your career to new heights.

End Game

Chapter 1

You will never reach the destination if the destination is unknown. –
Zaque Eyn

> ✓ Set Goals
> ✓ Career Plan
> ✓ Have a Direction

It's so easy for us to get caught up in the music or creation part of our career we forget all the other aspects of our profession and what is involved in reaching our goals. Most people think of only one aspect while neglecting to see all the other aspects that can help us get to where we want to go, making it impossible for longevity in the music industry.

I had a recent conversation with a potential client, eager to get an album created in order to play music live, and it got me thinking because one of the things said struck me quite odd; they didn't care about making money or charging for anything, at all, they just wanted to make an album so they could play and get signed to a record label. An interesting conundrum, I thought to myself; if they were never going to charge for gas, door sales, merchandise sales, CD's, nothing! How are they ever going to sustain a career and keep recording if they have no money to pay for those recordings? How are they ever going to get noticed by a record label if they have no sales to show the executives what they can do? How are they going to prove to anyone they have what it takes to make it? How are they going to track what areas and groups of people are into them?

Why would somebody be so concerned about making a CD if they were not planning on making any money from anything? Free CD's at shows - I don't see why not -, but no source of revenue, not even ticket sales? Sure, it's true we need something to give fans, or a potential club or booking agent to hear what we sound like and make a wise decision, and it's true we need things like an EPK to help us out, but do all of us really need all of these things at the same time?

The potential client somehow thought playing live would sustain their lives at one point, but in the mean time "we're not going to charge for anything, the record company will come to us." When I asked them what they wanted to get out of it, their response was "I just want to be in the industry, get signed, live the dream." I laugh silently, not because I think they are being silly or making a joke, but because I hear this so much from artists.

This conversation got me thinking about the Music Industry and why people don't succeed or ever make a real career out of music. The logical answer: no clear direction.

It seems as we get into our profession and figure out what we want to do, we don't clearly define what our end game is going to be with the proper steps in place to get us there. Is it playing live, like the potential client I was talking to, working in a famous studio or working with famous musicians? No matter what our end game is, we need to take appropriate steps, and put our game plan in place if we are ever going to have longevity in the business of music.

Most people don't have what it takes: passion, a real understanding, and road map of how to achieve realistic goals. No end game, defined goals in mind, or clear understanding of our market, means we are doomed to fail.

Like the potential client, you might be saying to yourself "All I need is live shows and a CD," but this is a completely wrong thought process. Set yourself up to be successful from day one, taking the right steps and making it work for you throughout the whole process. Remember it's the music business, so treat is as a business, because if you don't, you will not succeed.

The Short Check List:

- ✓ Homework and research
- ✓ Set goals to reach a 5 year goal
- ✓ Career plan in place
- ✓ Brand figured out
- ✓ Brand/Band registered as a business

With the right producer and engineer you can get professional sound with radio quality on just about any type of equipment now a days in any environment; Big Studios or small studios, Professional studios or home studios, it doesn't matter (it does but more on that later). How will the CD help you in the future or what will it do for your career right now? Plan and make the right choice today, and no regrets tomorrow. Find the best dam engineer you can for the budget you got, make the best EP you can for live show promotions or sales, put everything you got into it, heart & soul, even if it's for your family of four. If you've done it right, you will be proud of your accomplishment and perhaps sell it at shows or even on iTunes, and is the start of branding yourself while sticking in people's minds, which might lead to an eventual healthy career.

Not all of us are on the same path of course, some of us only want to play live or make a cd just to have, while others want to record music or produce bands for a living. By no means are these bad goals –your end game– too have, however, we need to dig deep to figure out what these are, and doing so will help us get to the point of financial stability from our craft, if that's what we're seeking. If we just start off playing live shows without our end game in mind we won't really grow, or worse, the show will be a disaster. You can't get into this line of work without pursuing your end game, taking the right steps to build a solid foundation for the future of your career, and must always be branding yourself.

When we fail to consistently brand ourselves without our end game in mind a stalemate situation happens, or worse, moving in the wrong direction and ruining good potential, or having to start from square one. If you're young enough, or have enough energy, you can start all over, but for most it means a regular 9-5 job for the rest of our years. Know it takes time, dedication, commitment, and does not happen over night. Have your end game in mind, strive towards the bigger, the better, each step of the way taking it up a notch every time, putting your style into it, and creating your future.

What Is Success?

Chapter 2

In one word: Dedicated…

- ✓ To-Do Lists
- ✓ Active Days
- ✓ Healthy Lifestyle
- ✓ Exercise and Meditation

People who see me as successful often ask about my success, and in talking with them, I find they see success for the wrong reasons. People deem success by earning lots of money or working for yourself, and never look at all the hard work involved. Successful people work very hard to get to the top of their game, therefore, it's important to define success and what it takes to be successful, because if we don't know what it means, or looks like, it is impossible to strive towards and achieve it.

"A great pleasure in life is doing what others say you cannot do" – Walter Bagehot

It's 5:30 am and my alarm goes off! Time to get up and start my cardio kickboxing session. I usually go to an Internet site that host's video's, which allows me to stay home, also saving money otherwise spent on classes. By 5:40am I am into my cardio kickboxing session.

6:40am and my kickboxing session is complete, I relax for a moment, catch my breath, and think of how great the rest of the day is going to be before taking a shower.

7am tea time. I love Yerba Mate and it's my favorite morning time pick me up, coffee is just so dirty to me... although I do go threw my times when I drink it, but mostly I'm all about the tea. I'll check my e-mail to see what's happened over night while asleep. If anything is important I respond immediately without hesitation. In between checking my e-mails I look at Twitter and various news sources to see what is going on in the world.

8:15am time to make some more tea and check craigslist for anything interesting that might suite a client of mine.

9am check to-do list and see what needs to happen today. I always have a to-do list, and since I got my iPhone am obsessed. From here it's time to tackle the important stuff first, things that need to get done *ASAP!* I'll proceed to make phone calls and send off any e-mail's I did not get to the night before or in my morning routine. (Since I constantly update and check my to-do list I know if I need to be checking it as soon as I wake up).

10am I am ready to get started with *"work,"* fortunately I do music for a living, and have a recording studio of my own, so working on music is effortless, and I don't really consider it work because I enjoy what I do.

12-1 pm time for lunch so I'll walk to the local market and grab a bite. I sometimes come back to the pad and chill out to some Food Network on the computer; I don't own a T.V., don't see any point wasting time with them or spending money on cable when the Internet is so vast. After lunch I'll continue working on music till 2 or 3pm ish. On the days I don't work on music, I'll work on projects for clients: marketing plans, event planning, marketing flyers, setting up flights, arranging times, etc. etc.

Around 3pm, when I am done with work, it's time to plan out my night. I'll check my e-mail and see who needs what and finish off any business stuff, then proceed to check the usual hot spots on my favorite websites, make calls to homies, and see what's going on for the night. I run an international podcast show and A&R for a radio station so there's always something worth checking out. Usually around 4pm I'll either get a call to do live sound at a club, or I'll have my night planned out with something fun in mind. If it's live sound, it works out great, because I have the opportunity to talk to the talent and see if they are recording, need a producer or an engineer, and offer to put them on my podcast show or be on the radio (if they are good of course, I have standards). If no gig, I'll fresh-in up a bit, maybe read a little, or do some more business stuff if I have deadlines to meet, before I head out.

7pm rolls around and it's out the door. Most likely I will link up with a home girl and grab a bite to eat while enjoying good conversation. Afterwards we'll take off to our chosen destination spot for the fun that will surely ensue. I try to make it home by 11 to 12, unless of course I am doing live sound and in this case it's usually 12:30am or later. At home I get ready for bed, bust out the relaxation App, and pass out. Then it's time to wake up and rock it all over again at 5:30am.

This is a typical day for me; I do a lot of yoga as well so I'll switch off cardio kickboxing with yoga. Maybe some days I will go for a hike, instead of going out in the nightlife... Am I perfect? No. Do I always wake up at 5:30am? No. However, I don't wake up any later than 6-7am as long as the gig or event the night before didn't go super late, and will never be up later than 8am even if I went to bed at 3am.

There are some key things I, and other successful people like me do to keep us going on this kind of routine.

Drugs & Alcohol: Don't do them. They only bring you down and slow you down. Believe it or not, the Rock Stars I know live my kind of life, not that one you hear about in the news. I am not saying we don't know how to have a good time or don't dabble now and again. What I am saying is that if you think it's party non-stop, 24/7, you're wrong. How you make a living as a professional in the entertainment world is by staying clean, with occasional exceptions, and live a similar type of routine you read above. If you have to ask or debate if it's a drug or not, the answer is yes! Yes it is. Anything that alters your mind, makes you lazy, or clouds your judgment and mind, is not going to help you stay motivated. You might be able to smoke that weed and mix a song, but when it comes time to do yoga or kickboxing and you are saying to yourself "I'm tired, I'll do it tomorrow," then you are doing you and you're career an injustice.

Exercise & Meditation: I am into yoga and meditation big time, and recently started cardio kickboxing. I have even started to get into the habit of doing both in the same day. Whether you want to do cardio kickboxing, yoga, work out at a gym, run, or whatever, it does not matter, what matters is that you get some form of exercise at least 3 days a week, 5 is best and 7 if you're a super star. It's amazing how much better you feel, and more things you get done in a day, when you exercise, and allows your mind to concentrate on tasks throughout the day along with releasing endorphins that stop stress in it's tracks.

Sleep: Most people won't wake up early right off the bat because it's hard. What you should do is set your alarm for an extra 10 minutes earlier than you did the day before. Do this until you are up 2 hours earlier then you are use to waking up, for most people that would mean 6 am you are up, and ready to rock. If you are getting proper exercise and eating right throughout the day your energy level will be so high that you won't need as much sleep as you are use to, and the few hours you do get will be amazing and restful like you've never known before.

Diet: I don't drink soda, or unnatural drinks. I drink water, real juice (natural, not pretend), kombucha, and tea. Occasionally I'll have coffee. I don't eat fast food, I eat as healthy as I can which means fruits, vegetables, organic, vegetarian, or locally raised and farm fresh meat not 100 or more miles away. No processed food, and I don't eat over 3,000 calories a day. I do my best to keep it at 2,000 calories a day, but a foodie at heart, when it's nighttime with the ladies I have to splurge now and again. Do I slip up? Yes. Do I beat myself up for it and say forget about all this healthy stuff? No! I don't. I get right back on track the next day. Every one of us needs to survive, so if I slip up because we are on tour and the only place to eat for 100 miles is a fast food place, and I'm starving, I'm going to eat. I will get the healthiest thing on the menu I can, simple as that. The thing is, when you actually eat healthy, the energy you get is phenomenal, last's longer, makes you feel amazing, your skin looks healthy, and you are less prone to sickness and diseases. Argue all you want, but until you experience this for yourself don't justify McDonald's as ok because you ate a salad with your big mac, large fries and 32oz soda for the 4th time this week. To get the benefits of a good diet, and start to feel great, you are going to need at least 2 weeks, if not 30 days, before your system is cleaned out from all the junk and you start to feel good. 90 days is when you are completely clean from all the junk and really reaping the maximum rewards, so stick with it and don't get discouraged.

Treat your body right, start from with-in and work out-word. I don't want to preach about yoga, but it changed how I feel: young, vibrant, energy level way over the top, and practicing since 2008. I am told I look in my 20's: I'm in my 30's. Diet, exercise and not doing drugs are something you have to stick with for at least 90 days before you really can see what I mean, but it's so worth it.

The last key component: **Taking things head on**. I have a can do attitude and know I can accomplish anything I set my mind to; doing things, hard and easy, always giving it my best and knowing my limitations along with who on my team can get it done. I'm not above saying I can't do something and asking for help if not my expertise. Like chemistry, I have somebody that can do this, and even if I didn't, I could find somebody because I'm resourceful. I see it as a challenge if something is hard, not a deterrent, and use this to push myself even harder.

So what is success? In a word: dedicated. Defined as: positive can do attitude, days full and rewarding, eating right, exercising, goals in mind, to-do lists, staying on top of your work, networking, looking out for other people and yourself. Once you realize this is success, and live a better lifestyle, financial rewards and freedom will naturally find you because you are on top of your game, living life to the fullest and everything else is just a side effect.

Food: an important part of how you feel, keep to a good diet and stay off the junk food; you're going to slip up, don't beat yourself up for it, get right back on track.

Drugs: If you do them, do them in moderation. Don't get caught up in big things like coke, speed or heroin. Weed is about all that is ok, and even then, sitting around all day smoking weed is lame, plus you won't have energy for anything else.

Alcohol: Just like weed. It's ok here and there but going out and getting drunk all the time, lame. It will make you feel like crap and not have energy to do the things you love and want to accomplish. Moderation people, that's all I can really say about that.

Entrepreneurship

Chapter 3

A strong will can accomplish anything. – Zaque Eyn

- ✓ Do I have what it takes?
- ✓ Is there a viable market for what I want to do?
- ✓ Is there going to be enough return on my investment?

As we embark on the journey of being entertainment professionals it is important to ask the hard questions, the lifestyle we are choosing is a long, and hard road. We are creative risk takers, and dedicated individuals; empowered.

Entrepreneurship involves countless amounts of time working on our craft, passion and profession; many nights will be spent working while others have fun, which will be hard at times. Relationships will suffer due to long hours working while trying to pay the bills, and those fortunate enough to not have too work spend even more time working on their business. So, before you become the entrepreneur, it is important to ask yourself three very important questions.

Do I have what it takes?

Is there a viable market for what I want to do?

Is there going to be enough return on my investment?

Take the time to answer these three questions seriously and thoughtfully. If you're a musician it might be easy to say, yes of course there is a viable market for Jazz music. But is it really? How many people do you know earning a living through Jazz music? Are they diversifying? This is not to suggest Jazz musicians don't make money, I personally know of several who do, however, someone else earning a living in a particular genre does not guarantee you anything. Chances are you'll have to do other things with music to create the living you're dreaming of: most likely giving voice lessons, or bass lessons, or writing sheet music for clients, and any number of other things to support yourself with music. The majority of working musicians diversify, and only a handful can actually say they just play for a living. The ones who do only play for a living might be diversifying: concerts, café gigs, street performing, weddings etc. The same is true for producers, sound engineers, managers, and event specialists. All these entities, and others I didn't mention, diversify their earning potential by doing more then just one thing. Sure the engineer might work in a studio, but moonlights as a live sound engineer to, likewise the producer might produce, but also engineers on the side. The point is to start thinking about the whole industry and not just a closed niche one, because the chances of surviving in one niche are slim. So I ask again, do you have what it takes? Is there a viable market for what you want to do? Is there enough return on your investment?

Goals and To-Do Lists

Chapter 4

I've never met a successful person without goals and to-do lists.

✓ Keep on track
✓ Reward yourself
✓ To-Do's everyday
✓ Have the bigger picture in mind

Setting goals is essential in creating realistic expectations and achieving success in your career. Goals are our road map for getting to where we want to go, and as we all know, without a road map we can get lost.

The thing about goals; they are just a tool and a guide. You should not be setting goals for yourself that are unrealistic and unattainable. Say you are making $900,000 a year and you have a goal to be making $1,000,000 by the end of next year. This is reasonable, you probably can reach this goal, if set up properly. On the other hand if you're only making $30,000 and the goal is making $1,000,000 by the end of next year, it's probably not realistic. Sure, you might have a product you're developing or working with a huge cooperation funding your project, and in this case it might be realistic. My point, however, you can't have a goal unlikely to happen in the time given. A more realistic goal in this case would be saying, *"In 5 years I want to be earning $1,000,000 instead of a years time,"* or *"Once I complete school in 3 years the job being offered to me starts out at $800,000 a year and with bonuses"*... You get my point.

The fun thing about goals is changing them, as we need to. If you don't achieve them by the time given, change the goal or extend the date. Life leads you on a different path sometimes and things happen that are out of our control. Never beat yourself up for not reaching a goal and celebrate when one is finished, always striving towards accomplishment.

All goals should have an end result with the small goals leading to the larger goals. Want to earn $1,000,000 in five year's time? What's it going to take to reach this goal? Start off with small daily goals that lead to the 3 month goals, and these 3 month goals lead to the 6 month goals which lead to the 1 year goals and so on. At the end of the year reflect on the past year, take an assessment of what was accomplished; went well, didn't go well, and don't forget to make your new goals.

Accomplish your goals and keep on track with these tricks I've learned over the years.

1. Make yourself 3 month, 6 month, 1 year, 2 year and 5 year goals.

2. Write them down on a piece of paper. Do not type them on a computer and print them out for the paper version. It is proven fact when we put pencil to paper, and physically write stuff out, we trigger our brain into making it more tangible, realistic, and achievable.

3. Put your hand written goals on a wall where they will be seen every day when you wake up and night before you go to bed. You are what you think about all day after all.

4. Make a to-do list every day and write them on a piece of paper. Keep it in your

pocket. With the advent of smart phones I actually put them in my phone. But be careful if you choose to do this. I personally check my phone all the time and constantly adding to my to-do tasks. Most of us using a phone will get lazy and stop updating tasks or putting in new ones. If you are like me and use your phone for a variety of things give it a shot, but just like the pencil to paper method, it does make it more tangible and achievable if you write them down on paper.

Crafting your to-do list:

Write down tasks to be done for the day, and go over goals to see what will get you closer to accomplishing them. My process.

1. I look at my week and consider what main things need to get done, make a note of specific days where something has to get done or be done by, then enter them into my daily to-dos for each day of the week.

2. I write everything down as is comes to me, even on the go.

3. I give myself priority marks so I know what is high priority versus low priority.

4. I look at my list and see if there are any times something has to be done by. This could be, "I need to get this song mixed by 5 pm tonight."

5. I then look at what can or has to be done before my highest priority. It's best to do high priority first, however, keep in mind the importance of time management, make sure deadlines are meet even with low priority.

6. My lowest priority: if I don't finish them today it's ok, transfer them over to tomorrow.

7. I continue to do these methods until my day and week are planned out.

8. Each time I complete a task it gets crossed off.

9. I think of a reward for the night and give it to myself if everything was completed for the day. Lately it's been a sweet treat, and since I love my sweet treats, I always make sure I get my to-dos done.

It's important to time manage properly as well. A lot of my to-dos I know how much time it will take to accomplish. Say I am doing yoga; I know it takes 1 hour or 1-1/2 hours depending on the routine for the day. Other tasks I may not know exactly how much time it will take, so I give myself plenty of time to accomplish them. Set aside an extra 30 minutes or an hour depending on the task if unsure. The high priority things get done no matter what.

The great thing about to-do list's, if I don't get a low priority task done it gets transferred over to the next day, keeping in mind the task may very well be a high priority the next day. To ensure I don't run into to many high priority tasks in one day, because of the transfer, I look at the week as a whole and time manage for such a scenario. Something needing completion by Friday I may start working on by Monday, allowing little things to get accomplish throughout the week for the task.

Making to-do lists helps create mini goals each day and week; in return the 3month, 6month, 1year and 5year goals become aligned for accomplishment.

One key fact: Each time an item is crossed off the to-do list I feel really good about myself for accomplishing something in the day, and what's more important than feeling good about yourself and accomplishing something?

Breaking Down Your Industry

Chapter 5

Understanding, defining and knowing will only make you greater. –
Zaque Eyn

✓ Know your genre
✓ Diversification is key
✓ Multiple jobs within the genre

Musicians, producers, engineers, and managers who want to be famous and/or be signed to a record label often converse with me; a subjective way of thinking, "I want to be famous," that does not really get down to the essence of what genre they are actually in and what is possible within it. Think about it like this, if you're a polka band, want to be famous, and get signed by a record label; name me 5 polka bands that are famous? Chances are you probably could name a couple, but realistically how many have Lady Ga Ga status? The answer is probably none. We have to look at our genre, and come to terms with it, because ultimately we need to know how we are going to achieve financial success, and what that success and fame looks like in it.

The key to earning a living with music is diversification, no matter the role or genre we choose. Producers, engineers, and managers have a higher rate of genre diversification then musicians because our skills can be used in many different situations as a whole, while musicians tend to stick with one style. It's important to know your strong points and weak points so you can use them to your advantage and diversify appropriately.

If you try and work in every genre, you might not get to the master level in each of them, because you are not spending enough time mastering one. A good way to approach your career is to learn what types of music you like working on and do whatever it takes to immerse yourself into them. I'm not saying working all different genres is a bad thing, or makes you any less effective at what you do, what I am saying is achieving success has a lot to do with how much time you spend with each genre. It is important to get yourself acquainted with the style of music you're working with: going to clubs, concerts, parties, networking events, industry seminars, music stores, and listening to music; all things we need to do to educate and immerse ourselves into the genre, and extremely important. We can't expect to succeed if we don't understand the scene, and know what is trending and not trending. Knowing what they did in the 80's doesn't mean anything if you don't know what they are doing today.

Knowing your genre will also help you understand how far you can go within that genre. The pop genre, for instance, has the potential to be world famous with TV, billboards, radio and the like. The folk genre is not going to have the same level of stardom or exposure. I'm not saying you can't achieve stardom in folk music; anything is possible if you set your mind to it, but be realistic for your genre of choice. By looking into the scene you can get the tools you'll need to go down the right path, making the right decisions along the way, while understanding how far you can potential go.

Pop music has a certain way of doing things that is completely different from the punk scene. We need to look at more then just the music to be effective at what we hope to accomplish. What are the words being used in the genre? Is slang what makes things interesting in that genre? Is slang looked down upon in the genre? What are the clothes people wear? How do people act? Are people into motorcycles and old cars? Can you improve anything? Can you do anything different? What are they doing that is making them money? How are their songs structured that people fall in love with? Breaking down these types of things will step your game up ten fold when working in the genre.

Whether you're producing, engineering, managing, or playing the music, you'll want to make sure you are keeping in the means of the genre. I think bands can attest to this the most; if you walk into a punk show wearing an Armani suit you are going to stand out like a sore thumb. Likewise, if you're in a punk band wearing an Armani suit, people are going to be like "what the fuck!" Of course, if in your performance while playing your song, *Fuck the Man*, you rip it apart and tear it up, then you'll be the highlight of the show and people will be like, exactly! Fuck the corporate world! But most of us can't afford $1,500 suites every time we play a song on stage. The same is true when working on music, you got to know what works and what doesn't work, and adjust, because if you're producing, engineering, or managing, you have to coach the band appropriately, and the band has to know what is right for them. If the band starts singing about *Fuck the Man*, and they are folk musicians, everyone should be asking, "How is this relevant to the genre?" Certain words might not be used in a particular genre, so you might need to suggest a word change in the song to keep it relevant. Likewise the band will be able to better construct an image, brand, and songs, if they know the in's and out's of the genre.

Knowing the genre you're choosing to work with has advantages when out networking as well. When I go to a punk show I don't wear my fancy sport coat, I put on jeans and a t-shirt. I don't want to stand out in the crowd or be "that guy." If you're going to scout for new talent and you are not fitting the part then chances are the band is not going to trust you because you already don't get it. I'm not saying don't be yourself, but if you go to a punk show in a suite and tell the band you want to produce them, they are going to laugh at you, maybe not in your face, but they will.

I teach industry people: producers, engineers, managers, and musicians, how to own their particular genre with the things we just talked about. Part of what I show them, not just the break down of their genre and understanding it, is learning how to use this to an advantage. In order to use this to your advantage let's go over some useful tactics.

One thing we do is to really looking into what is going on in their genre, making notes, and creating go-to-list for hot points. These notes are just simple things: clothes, trends, music style, studio techniques, song structures, vocals, words used, etc. etc. This allows us to pick apart everything, and see what is working and not working for brands or bands. Once we have the list we can start to put together a plan.

Sometimes, after the break down, we have to change the whole way they are doing things. Maybe they have to go out and get new clothes, or realize by not going to punk shows and only going to pop shows, is the reason why they are not getting punk artists; because they don't know the scene.

What we do is look at our assessment of the genre, note what's not happening in their genre, and use this to our advantage. Maybe this genre is not using any kind of blogs to keep people informed of shows coming up or just doing what it is blogs do, informing. Perhaps it is wise to start a blog and over time it will become the standard for information in that genre. This isn't really going to be true, creating a blog, for: punk, pop, rock, or any other popular genre, however, there is always a new form of music that no body really knows about that has yet to be discovered on a scale outside of your hometown. Maybe the genre isn't embracing podcast shows; perhaps they could start a local podcast show that highlights and get's everyone in the genre involved. This also means you are creating your own network within this genre that makes you more of the go to person rather then just another sideliner. By breaking down the genre, we can start to find niches that can be capitalized on.

It shouldn't always be about money either. Your network is your strongest attribute and should be your main focus at all times. It's all about your network!

Some genres will get you to the movies faster then other ones, and so what if your genre only has 2,000 people in it right now? Use that, get involved in it, and help define it. Get to know everyone of those people and build yourself a very strong network. This is the essence of being famous, knowing everyone in your genre.

Having your whole genre exited about what you're doing and participating in what you're doing, is in essence, being famous, and we need to remember this throughout our entire career. Look at the podcast scenario. If we started off charging people to listen and be on the show you'll never break into the scene because you're not established, but if it's free and you are donating your time to make it happen, you'll end up having to turn people away till the next show because you're so popular. When you do get to the charging point, you'll never do it. Why? Because you are getting so much residual work from it that charging isn't important anymore, besides, it was about networking and building up your community in the first place, right?

Do selfless acts of kindness as a general rule of thumb; this is the final thing I show my clients. If you're just starting out as a producer, and asking $5,000 to produce one song, nobody is going to pay you, in fact you could be ruining your credibility for future requests. We have to start small and work our way up. If you get to know everyone of those 2,000 people, and you do it because you've built a blog, podcast, or whatever; when it's time to have a show, ask if anyone needs a producer, or your album just came out, you will have 2,000 people who are all possibly interested. Selling your album at $5 to 2,000 people adds up to $10,000 and that's pretty dam good.

Stick to knowing your genre and understanding it, strive to help it, and implement fresh ideas. I'd rather the whole folk scene know who I am, respect me, and always want to work with me no matter what, versus no body knowing who I was because I couldn't focus. Once we accomplish our mission of immersing ourselves into our genre of choice and becoming well know in it, if it's record labels you want, they will come... they won't have a choice not to.

Remember it's ok to work in multiple genres and aspects of the industry, diversification is key, we just have to be realistic in what we are trying to get out of it, and accomplish in it, for it to work for us.

Do's & Don'ts of Listening

Chapter 6

It is important for us to give the same respect as we wish to receive. – Zaque Eyn

✓ Don't interrupt
✓ Adopt a positive attitude
✓ Withhold judgment until speaker is finished

The do's and don'ts of listening is a quick guide in conducting yourself when listening to other people. The idea stems from listening to a speaker talk, but as I have learned in my years of networking, these are tips for every day life. You should use these as a guideline and a starting point in how to conduct yourself around others and make better information collecting choices.

Listening well to the other person shows them respect, allows you to receive all the information, and allows you to make educated responses by not cutting them off in the middle of a conversation. If they have not completed the thought, and you cut them off, you don't allow proper communication, and can have negative repercussions; they may want to leave the conversation and stop talking with you. When you cut someone off, or do not pay attention, what you are saying to him or her is you don't care, and "I am more important then you are."

Listening shows the other person you respect and see their point; even if you don't like what they are saying, or care for their point, it allows us to hear the whole argument before we put our two sense in. They may even answer a question we had because we allowed the entire thought to be completed.

Beyond this, listening allows us to give off that professional touch that is unspoken but understood; it makes us seem more like we know what we are doing in the other person's eyes, and therefore, gives us an edge over the person who keeps cutting them off. If you were in a meeting using these techniques, and that person had another meeting where they were cut off constantly, you will be the one remembered as professional and the person to work with.

It is important for us to give the same respect as we wish to receive.

Do's of Listening

Do adopt the attitude that you will always have something to learn.

Do take time to listen, give the speaker your full attention, and hear the speaker out.

Do withhold judgment until the speaker is finished. Strive to locate the main ideas of the message.

Do try to determine the work meanings in the context of the speaker's background. Listen for what is being implied, as well as what is being said.

Do establish eye contact with the speaker. Read body language. Smile, nod, and give an encouraging sign when the speaker hesitates.

Do ask questions at appropriate times to be sure you understand the speaker's message.

Do restate the speaker's idea at appropriate moments to make sure you have received it correctly.

Don'ts of Listening

Don't listen with only half an ear by "tuning out" the speaker and pretending you are listening.

Don't unnecessarily interrupt the speaker or finish the speaker's statement because of impatience or wanting to respond immediately.

Don't fidget or doodle while listening.

Don't let other distractions bother you and the speaker.

Don't confuse facts or opinions.

Don't show disapproval or insensitivity to the speaker's feelings.

Don't respond until the speaker has said what he or she wants to say.

Don't become defensive.

Understanding the Company

Chapter 7

Knowledge is key to success. – Zaque Eyn

✓ Influence
✓ Understand
✓ Build Rapport

As a Professional Entertainment Brand, YOU INC., it is important to understand your particular niche, industry, clients and the competition. Without the right tools and knowledge, an initial contact is like rolling the dice. In order to be more effective and achieve higher success rates, we'll need to do a couple of things before we start contacting people.

Keeping up to date on your industry is essential to your career and why it ranks first, but this one should be a given. If you are reading this book chances are you're using the Internet, on at least one device, daily. If you spend some time each day learning something, anything new, when it comes time to talk with a client, you will have some working knowledge in your bag of tricks, proving helpful to your cause, instead of, that high score you just got on your favorite game racing through your mind. Don't get so caught up in your own thing that you forget to check into the real world every now and again either.

Keep a writing utensil/paper, smart gadget, handy when doing daily research or are in the process of doing client and company research. You'll want to make notes of important things and be able to reference those at all times…

Record Label Boss is never, ever, ever to be called Rob

Best chord structure for pop music is E, B, C#m, A

The next big thing in the industry right now is… ?

Not taking notes, a simple little thing, leaves you stuck hunting all over the place, and the Internet, again, trying to remember information you came across in the worst possible moments.

Stages in Understanding

Stage 1: *Problem Recognition:* Problem recognition occurs when a company realizes that their current state of affairs differs significantly from some ideal state.

Influencers:

- Change in financial status (i.e. a job promotion or industry change, etc.)
- Change in company characteristics (i.e. new division, etc.)
- Normal depletion (i.e.; no more new artists coming in to company, etc.)
- Product or service performance (i.e. older gear in the studio etc.)
- Past decisions (i.e. didn't & still don't embrace the internet like "we" should, etc.)
- Availability of products (i.e. introduction of a new service or product, etc.)

An Entertainment professional must understand the problem recognition stage in order to decide on the appropriate; marketing, branding, interviewing, strategy to use.

Stage 2: *Information Search and Evaluation:* The second stage involves collection and evaluation of appropriate information from both internal and external sources. The principle objective is to establish evaluative criteria – the features or characteristics of the product or service that the company will use to compare brands.

Stage 3: *Brand Decision:* Once companies have evaluated your brand in their evoked set and made their choice, they must still decide when the time is right to make their choice and work with you.

Stage 4: *Post-Brand Evaluation:* The company decision-making process does not end with them hiring you. Small brands, yourself, that desire repeat gigs or work from the companies need to understand post-brand behavior.

Post-Brand dissonance (conflict) *is a type of cognitive dissonance, a tension that occurs immediately following a booking decision when companies have second thoughts as to the wisdom of the person hired. This anxiety is obviously uncomfortable for companies and can negatively influence brand evaluation and satisfaction.*

Psychological Influences

Company's needs are never completely satisfied, thereby ensuring the continued existence of business. One of the more complex characteristics of needs is the way in which they function together in generating behavior. In other words, various needs operate simultaneously, making it difficult to determine which need is being satisfied by specific product or service. Nevertheless, careful assessment of the needs-behavior connection can be very helpful in developing marketing and branding strategy. Different hiring of the same type of brand satisfies different needs. For example, companies hire different producers for different genres they need to have recorded. But they also hire different producers based on their expertise and years of working knowledge. A needs-based strategy would result in a different marketing or branding approach in each of these situations.

Needs: Needs are often described as the starting point for all behavior. Without needs, there would be no behavior. Although company's needs are innumerable, they can be identified as falling into four categories – physiological, social, psychological, and spiritual.

Perceptions: A second psychological factor, perception, encompasses those individual processes that ultimately give meaning to the stimuli confronting companies. When this meaning is severely distorted or entirely blocked, companies perception can cloud a brands marketing or branding effort and make it ineffective. For example, a company might mark its studio sessions "on discount" to communicate a way for up and coming musicians to get professional recording, but brands perceptions may be that "this studio is suffering."

Perception is a two-sided coin. It depends on the characteristics of both the stimulus and the perceiver. Companies attempt to manage huge quantities of incoming stimuli through perceptual categorization, a process by which things that are similar are perceived as belonging together. Therefore, if a brand wishes to position it's service alongside an existing brand and have it accepted as comparable, the marketing mix or branding efforts should reflect an awareness of perceptual categorization. Similar quality can be communicated through similar prices or through a website design with a color scheme similar to that of an existing brand. These techniques will help a company fit the new brand into their desired category of interest and implementation into the company.

If a company has a strong loyalty to a brand, it is difficult for other brands to penetrate perceptual barriers. This company is likely to have distorted images of competing brands because of a pre-existing attitude. Company's perceptions thus present a unique communication challenge.

Motivations: Unsatisfied needs create tension within a company. When this tension reaches a certain level, the company becomes uncomfortable and is motivated to reduce the tension.

Everyone is familiar with hunger pains, which are manifestations of the tension created by an unsatisfied physiological need. What directs a person to obtain food so that the hunger pains can be relieved? The answer is motivation. Motivations are goal-directed forces that organize and give direction to tension caused by unsatisfied needs. Brands cannot create needs, but they can offer unique motivations to companies. If an acceptable reason for hiring a brand is provided it will probably be internalized by the company as a motivating force. The key for the brand is to determine which motivations the company will perceive as acceptable in a given situation. The answer is found through an analysis of other company behavior variables.

Like physiological needs, the other three classes of needs – social, psychological, and spiritual – can be similarly connected to behavior through motivations. For example, when incomplete satisfaction of a company's social needs is creating tension, a brand may show how it's service can fulfill those social needs by providing acceptable motivations to that company. A brand might provide networking opportunities via gatherings that a company may be interested in and cannot do without.

Understanding motivations is not easy. Several motivations may be present in any situation, and they are often subconscious. However, they must be investigated in order for the brand's effort to be successful.

Attitudes: Like other psychological variables, attitudes cannot be observed, but everyone has them. Do attitudes imply knowledge? Do they imply feelings of good or bad, favorable or unfavorable? Does an attitude have direct impact on behavior? The answer to each of those questions is a resounding yes. An attitude is an enduring opinion, based on a combination of knowledge, feeling, and behavioral tendency.

An attitude may act as an obstacle or a catalyst in bringing a company to a brand. For example, companies with the belief that a local, independent run brand (record label, recording studio, etc.) has lower quality then an established brand may avoid the local brands. Armed with an understanding of the structure of a particular attitude, a brand can approach the company more intelligently.

Sociological Influences

Culture: In marketing and branding yourself, culture means the behavioral patterns and values that characterize a group of customers in a target market. These patterns have a significant impact on the selection of choosing your brand. It is easy to overlook the cultural variable because its influences are so neatly embedded in our society. Culture is somewhat like blinking your eyes. You don't think about it, or its function, until you get something in your eye.

The nature of culture should concern the brand in search of more clients and/or work. Cultural norms are apparent in all business and it is very important to understand each culture you are working with or going to be working with. Different behaviors mean different things in different cultures, and because of this a simple mistake can mean no work or the right behavior could land you your biggest client. However, because cultural norms change, it is important to keep up with trends and norms in a particular culture as they can change every couple of years.

An investigation of culture within a narrower boundary – defined by age, religious preference, ethnic background, or geographical location – is called *subcultural analysis.* In this type of learning you should note, that like in culture, subcultural analysis can change from group to group. Like in America where the younger generation may have a slang word for something, like *totes*, the older generation may not understand the meaning. It is important to know and understand whom you are working with in order to act appropriately.

Social Class: Another sociological factor that effects decisions and behavior is social class. Social classes are divisions within a society having different levels of social prestige. The social class has very important implications to marketing your brand. Different lifestyles correlate with different social prestige, and as you can image, different products can give the illusion of, or put you in, a certain social class. $250,000 Bentley verses a Pinto verses a Smart car.

Occupation is probably the most significant indicator of social class. But other indicators such as school, income, and your possessions, will also determine your social class. So when you are building up your brand you have to determine first, what social class you want to belong to. Obviously, if say, you're an aspiring sound engineer, you will never be put in a social class of prestige like that of the CEO of Warner Bros. However, this does not mean you can't hang with the big boys and become their friend and be a part of their social class. This brings us to point two, being an upstanding person. You can never expect to be a part of another social class, especially in the entertainment industry, if you don't get "it."

Reference Groups: This could really be a part of social class, but it does have a point that deserves it's own section. Reference groups are groups that a company allows to influence their behavior. The challenge is in understanding how this can help your brand land the gig or job and to understand the company and what they are doing.

Companies tend to accept group influence because of their perceived value and benefits. Without group influence, a record label like Warner Bros would have never decided to work with rock music back in the day. It just finally got to the point they could no longer avoid it; having seen groups of people eat up the music. It became a necessity to support it other wise they'd be missing out on all the extra money. These perceived benefits give the influencers various kinds of power. Five widely forms of power, all available to your brand, are: reward, coercive; referent, expert; and legitimate power.

> **Reward and Coercive power** relate to a groups ability to give and to withhold rewards. Rewards can be material or psychological. Recognition and praise are typical psychological rewards.
>
> **Referent and Expert power** involve neither rewards nor punishments. They exist because a company attaches great importance to being like the group, or perceives the group as being knowledgeable. Referent power influences a company to conform to a group's behavior or select and buy products the groups use or has (depending on the influence of the group).
>
> **Legitimate power** involves summoning what the company ought to do. We are familiar mostly with this at a cultural level, where it is evident in the nature of the culture.

Opinion Leaders: Opinion leaders are group members playing a key communications role. These people are generally knowledgeable and visible.

Personal versus Business Rapport

To work with other business professionals you must be willing to build business rapport. Business rapport is different than personal rapport. We must understand the difference between the two in order to be successful in our careers. If you master the art of building business rapport, your career, financial horizons, and overall success in business will be as good as guaranteed. If you master the art of personal rapport, then you'll widen your social circle of influence and interpersonal network, and you'll find greater opportunities, resources, and personal fulfillment in just about every corner of your life. Let's take a closer look so you can understand them.

Business Rapport: When you build effective business rapport with other professionals, and the decision makers, you're building platinum hit after hit where ideas once existed in your basement. You're tapping into their greater influence and authority and you're multiplying your results accordingly. One of the key words here is "effective," which should not be confused with "efficient." Being efficient is having the ability to do whatever needs to be done as fast as possible. Being effective is making sure that whatever needs to be done is getting done the best it can be. This difference is extremely important in a business relationship. For instance, if you try and build business rapport to quickly, it will not have the crucial ingredients of loyalty and strength needed to withstand the many ups and downs that will surly ensue. Inadequate rapport built in haste will simply not last.

Personal Rapport: Good solid personal rapport is built on the basis of mutual understanding and appreciation for another person's point of view, culture, feelings, and whatever else the person stands for or happens to be headed to. The art of mirroring usually falls into the personal rapport category.

As professionals we must separate business and personal rapport. If our efforts happen to build strong personal rapport, that's great! But we should focus first on business rapport. Once you have mastered both of these you can start to implement both techniques in every situation. Think of it like adding salt and pepper to food. A little bit of both really makes the food pop! But too much of either and the food no longer is good.

Here are some things to avoid when building business rapport:

1. *Ice breaking.* Get straight to the point and save the small talk for after you've discussed what it is your contacting them for in the first place. If it's a meeting for engineering an album, and you only have 5 minutes to talk with the person, asking them about the Grammy on their desk will most likely take up your whole meeting as they explain the story. Don't let yourself fall in to this. Stick to your agenda. They will appreciate it and you will accomplish the meeting you set out to have.

2. *Overstating and under-delivering of anything.* It's ok to openly and honestly fail at something. But it's never ok to knowingly set a false expectation by making inflated or exaggerated statements. Your business rapport relies heavily on your honesty, integrity, and ability to deliver on your promises as well as exceed the expectations you have set.

3. *Criticizing anything or anyone's efforts.* Be careful and respectful. Making a statement like, "Who wired this studio? It looks like a tangled mess," could land you in hot water when they reply, "My son." Don't let yourself fall into this mistake.

4. *Telling a trade secret or sharing "confidential" or "company private" information.* If you show or say anything to someone that you don't have the authority to show or say, you won't earn any points of trust. The question will always become: What's stopping you from betraying their confidence and trust in you to someone else?

5. *Assuming that business rapport will carry over to personal rapport.* Personal rapport takes certain liberties that may no be acceptable or reasonable in a business relationship, in the initial phases. Some individuals lead very personal lives and do not want the two worlds to intertwine. You must honor this if it's the case.

6. *Showing up late for anything.* Being late sends a clear message that you place two values on the other person's time: little and none.

7. *Procrastination of any kind.* Similar to being late, procrastination tells the other party that you have let some other activity, or no activity at all, take priority over the business relationship.

8. *Negative talk about anyone or anything.* Just don't do it. People can be enemies at one moment and the best of friends another. Don't get caught up in gossip or putting someone else down. If you don't have anything nice to say about someone, then don't say anything at all.

9. ***Saying you know someone or something when you don't.*** You are taking a huge risk and can/will get caught. It's a bad idea so stay away from it.

10. ***Asking for a favor before you've earned the right to that favor.*** This is greed at it's finest, or worse, hour. When it comes to business rapport, it's always best to have the other person offer a favor rather than prematurely ask for one. Better yet, offer something up first with no favor in return.

What you must always do to build effective business rapport:

1. *Make the best first impression possible.* You only get one chance to make a first impression. There are two parts to this: A) What they hear, see, and/or feel during the first few seconds of your interaction with them B) What they hear, see, and/or feel during the last few seconds of your interaction with them.

2. *Consistently exceed expectations.* Credibility is the cornerstone of strong, lasting business rapport. The fastest way to build credibility is to do what you say you'll do and be willing to go the extra mile beyond that. In order to succeed, you must exceed.

3. *Make yourself an appreciating asset.* Like any other great investment, you must increase in value over time without them having to make a greater investment in you. You must continue to bring in fresh new ideas, greater information, and enhanced services to the table—and whatever you bring, "it" and "you" must increase in perceived value.

4. *Position yourself as someone who is indispensable.* This goes hand in hand with becoming an appreciating asset. You need to be someone who can't be replaced by your competition.

5. *Make your self-improvement apparent.* Never let yourself become intellectually, emotionally, or physically stagnant. You must constantly seek ways to increase your personal and business value. Read trade-specific books, articles and blogs. Find ways to expand your knowledge and demonstrate that you are upwardly mobile.

6. *ALWAYS BE UPBEAT!* Everyone appreciates a winning attitude. Maintain an uplifting mood, attitude, and opinions, and you will be appreciated as the person who knows how to make the best of any situation. Enthusiasm and positive outlook will take you a long way.

7. *Dress for success.* This is a very important part of building business rapport. Success has an aura all its own, and you can take on that aura with the tasteful way you dress. Dress the part that the other person is in. If they wear suites, don't show up in shorts or sagging pants below your knees.

8. *Speak with an appropriate vocabulary.* The proper use and understanding of words can provide us with the tools we need to make the best possible first impression and build excellent business rapport.

9. ***Become a useful team player.*** You must be looked upon as an asset, not a liability. Business rapport is established and grows on the basis that a contribution is being made without the other person asking for that contribution. That's what Team Work is all about.

10. ***Listen intently.*** That means listening with undivided attention, focus, and understanding.

Persuasive Skills

Chapter 8

Manipulation isn't what you think. –Zaque Eyn

- ✓ Space
- ✓ Body Language
- ✓ One handshake to rule them all

Body language is such an important part of how we interact with one another, we need to understand how to use it properly in order for us to excel. Once you have mastered body language, along with business rapport, you will be able to build better working relationships, land great jobs, and get solid clients.

We might not pick up on a head tilt, or someone doing exactly what we are doing, but it does grab our subconscious. Masters at the craft of body language are capable of getting ahead farther in life because the people they talk to are more likely to be at ease and agreeable with them.

Mastering body language is not simply learning how to do it and applying it, but also knowing how to use the techniques to your advantage in a given situation. For instance, when you learn how to mirror someone, and use it properly, they will follow your lead instead of the other way around. Mirroring someone gets you in rhythm with one another, which is the goal of this technique. Once you have achieved the rhythm, they will see you as a peer, making it more plausible they will want to work with you because now it seems you are the same type of person as them. However, just applying this technique without follow-through of the other techniques outlined in this section, or failure to use the rest of the techniques in this book, could prove to be a huge mistake on your part.

In this section I will be going over the art of body language, and breaking down some key components of how to manipulate your situation. Be WARNED! These techniques are NOT something done on an important person until you have solid business rapport and mastered the craft of body language, or are at least comfortable making these techniques appear as if you are not doing them. You MUST practice on friends or family so if you get caught you're not hurting your relationship with a client or potential client. These techniques are a way to increase your chances of success and should be used with caution and care. Done right, you can go further then you ever have before, done wrong and you could end up nowhere.

Signals

"Yes" Styles:

Open palms towards you

Leaning forward

Smiling

Direct body orientation

Head nodding

Enhanced eye contact

"No" Styles:

Folded arms

Tapping

Hand holding their chin up

Feet and body pointed in different directions other then yours

Hands on the knees or over the mouth

Intensified fidgeting

Constant eye movement that's not at you

Shaking their head

Maybe Styles:

Taking a sip of a drink

Biting the tip of their glasses or pencil or pen

Cleaning their glasses

Scratching their head

Use these styles to find out if the other person is picking up on what you're trying to convey and see if they are into you and your conversation. It also works in reverse to give them subconscious signals that, you may or may not be into, what they are trying to convey.

Remember, while these styles mostly fall into the categories I have provided, not all of them simply mean yes or no. The arm cross for instance might be because it is cold outside and they are trying to keep warm, or it's just how they stand and talk. If a combination of 3-4 yes's happen, it is safe to say that it is probably a yes, likewise with the no or maybe. The important thing to remember is judging each situation for what it is and using your best understanding of why something might be happening.

Mirroring the other person

This all-important technique helps you to build rapport with the other person in an extremely fast amount of time. Mirroring the other person is exactly what it sounds like; we are imitating the other person's body movements and matching them to our own. This technique will allow you to be seen as an equal in the other person's eye. It can help you convey your point, get jobs or build new friendships. When you have mastered this technique it will also help you control your situation, get what you want, and gain the respect you seek. This is something that you should practice until you get it down before you use this in a situation that matters.

There are lots of things people do when you talk to them. Some fold their arms; some breath heavy or soft and others talk really fast or really slow. You have to pick up on these traits and mirror them so you are doing the same thing, a master will pick up on these in under a second.

Remember; use these techniques sparingly and sparsely. The point of these techniques is to build report and get on the same "level" as the other person without them knowing what you're doing.

Let's get into some finer details of mirroring another person.

Body movements: Body movements can be things like folded arms, arms by the side, body turned away from you, hands move when they talk, hands folded when they are talking or making a point, hands to their nose, hands to their mouth and similar type gestures.

You'll want to use discretion when using this technique or mirroring. It is important to fine-tune what you want to do by not seaming obvious. So don't do everything they are doing all at once, they will catch on and call you out on it.

Part of what you want to do is learn what they are doing instantly when you talk to them.

Say you go into a meeting with a person and every time they make a point their hands come together, fingers touching, but no palms touching. From this point on, every time you go to make a point you do the same thing. In the other persons subconscious mind you will be seen as someone who is on the same page, or on the "level". This technique uses what you have learned from them to your advantage, and conveys the same message; "I to am making a point." Of course this is not something you do exactly when they are.

Let's take a look at the arm cross. When talking to someone and they cross their arms in mid conversation with you, go into your mirror mode and do the same thing. If they un-cross their arms after a bit, you do the same. Don't do this at the same exact second, wait a second or two but not a minute or two. This mirror style, and pretty much all of them, can be used for any movement of the body. Be careful, it is important to pick certain traits to mirror, but not all, as you run a high risk of getting caught in the act.

Once you have started to mirror a person, and are in rhythm with one another, you can start to change the rhythm how you want. Mirroring taps into the subconscious and translates into: what you do they will follow; their body has become comfortable with you, and without knowing it, wants to stay in rhythm with you, and vice versa.

Say you want to stop crossing your arms, once you're in rhythm you can start to do something else like lower your arms to your side, chances are the other person will follow and do the same. If you decided to start blinking more then usual they may just start doing the same.

Don't fool yourself though, not everything you do the other person will follow. Sometimes after you've taken the lead, in the rhythm, they might start to go back to their own, and this is perfectly ok and normal. However, it is wise to continue to mirror them in order the keep your rhythms in sync if this has happened.

You have to be careful when using techniques like these, other then the reasons already expressed, because you will have to use this every time you see them. Not to say every time you see them you have to do everything the same, but if mirroring one time and not another, something will seem off. It is wise to use it sparingly and intelligently. Pick one or two things to mirror you can keep up with all the time whenever you see them. This way you still remain an individual, but a peer at the same time.

Talking: If a person is talking slow, it is extremely important to talk at the same pace. If you are a fast talker, spend time talking slow on cue, or if you're a slow talker practice boosting the energy in your voice to keep up with fast talkers. The person who talks slow will not be able to understand a fast talker, and surprisingly the reverse is also true, a fast talker will get frustrated and think less of someone who talks to slow, possibly seeing you as unintelligent. Moreover it could make you seem too edgy and not have much authority. You don't want them to think you are a not a person who would work out as a client or company because of something so simple, but it happens more often then not.

Eye's: Eye movement is another important mirror technique. If the other person is constantly looking away from you it means they are uninterested in what you are saying, for the most part anyways. While this is not a good situation to be in, you can get back their attention by mirroring them. Go ahead and start looking where they are looking when they look away, as if you were both looking at a nice car off in the distance. Subconsciously they will start to pick up on this and direct more of their attention towards you. Of course they might not direct their attention towards you, but if you are using all the techniques in this section you will find they are more captivated by you then not.

It is important to look directly into the eyes of the other person when talking, but it could get a little creepy to hold a conversation with someone for 5 minutes while staring into their eyes the whole time. What you'll want to do; find a secondary point on their face, close to their eyes, to look at every once in a while. A good rule of thumb is about every 20-30 seconds look at your secondary point. A secondary point might be the nose, cheek or lips.

Breathing: Another great tool in your arsenal: breathing. By bringing your breathing to the same rate as the other person, you put yourselves in harmony with one another. This technique is really helpful in getting the other person to feel calm and relaxed around you, more secure and agreeable. A bit tricky if you're not use to it; you can't get right up on them to hear how they are breathing after all, that would be weird. Pay close attention to their body language and chest, careful if it's a woman and you are a man, as it should help you adjust your breathing to theirs. This should be very low key on your end, and not in any way obvious. By mastering this technique you can amplify the use of body movement allowing you to be in perfect rhythm with one another.

Smile Factor (Social Smile): Smiling is a great way to let people feel welcome in your presence, comfortable around you, and can spark conversations. Practice smiling in a mirror for the best, real, and genuine smile possible. Have your smile face on whenever you go out of the house. Every time you meet eyes with a stranger, smile at them. You'd be surprised at how good you feel, and make the other person feel. Smiling keeps you in a great mood which people pick up on, and opens up a whole new world when you smile at everyone.

Respecting Each Others Space

When talking to another person, consider the space in between both of you. Avoid breeching personal space and making them uncomfortable; if you do, all bets are off.

4 different kinds of space to be considered: public, social, personal, and intimate.

Public: This area is twelve to twenty-five feet or more. Public space is not really in your control, but you can do things to make it work for you. When you walk into a group setting, or conference room full of people, allow your energy, and enthusiasm to shine. Walk in with your shoulders held back and high, your head held high, and have your best social smile showing. Take time to look around the room and meet the eyes of others to determine who are the more powerful authority people in the room. You will come across as someone people want to know and talk to, as well as, seeing who the confident one's are and aren't. This allows you to be open to the right people both mentally, and how you project yourself outward.

Social: Think of this as the beach blanket zone: approximately 4 feet zones from one another. People who want to get approval will move in to about 4 feet away, while those who are not trying to gain approval will move about 8 feet away. You can use this space to judge if the other persons into the conversation, idea or venture, especially when it comes to closing a deal or landing a client. You have to be careful crossing over into personal space if it is unwanted, so I suggest following their lead into the personal space zone. The reason being, if you are successful in everything else up until this point, not only will they want to be on a good friendship level, but as a way to show you are accepted.

Personal: Considered the friendship zone: ranges from 2 to 4 feet of space and generally reserved for family members or really good friends. You shouldn't be in this zone right away with someone you've just met. A club or music venue space more likely then not: you have to be close. We all have our own personal space we like, so be careful not to invade others. Signs you have invaded their space include: leaning away, increased blinking, decrease in smiling, crossed arms, sitting up straight, turning away, blushing.

Intimate: This is a touching space: from your body to about 2 feet away and reserved for family, very close friends and children. You should never be in this space unless your reserved group applies. In some cases you might need to be in this space, like when you're at an over-packed show or on the subway, the type of situation where you have no other choice; it would be deemed ok. But be forewarned, if you get into this space with someone not in your reserved group or in a situation where you have no choice, you run the risk of making the other person very, very, very uncomfortable.

The Only Handshake you'll ever need:

Go toward the person, lean in slightly forward, look them in the eye, extend your right hand so that your right side is parallel to the ground while at the same time introducing yourself. Make sure to use your whole hand. Your grip should feel comfortable and at ease with the same pressure as if you were going to be holding hands together, yet firm. All of your body parts should be facing towards them. Keeping your thumb straight up will ensure a good handshake. The whole handshake should last no longer than couple of seconds. Your elbow should be slightly bent, this means that you are not to far away from them but you are also not invading their space. Two pumps with you hand should do the job. Avoid using more then two pumps, three at the most. If they continue to pump their hand with you, continue but assert some personal authority and pull away after 5.

It is hard trying to explain the complicatedness of having that special something people see in you that stands out from the rest. So I will offer up some friendly advice. I am constantly told I have "it," that special something that just stands out from the masses. The most solid advice I can give you is: **stay true to yourself, hold the utmost respect for others, have an extremely high level of integrity and be extremely ethical.** Don't get discouraged. With time it's possible to put yourself into a better "it" category. Get a mentor, hang out and be friends with successful people, and ditch your weed buddies. **Success breeds success,** and trust me when I say it will rub off on you if you're around it. Of course there is so much more to the "it" factor, however, just by reading this book and the successful understanding and implementation of it's tool's will guarantee you a spot in this category.

Writing Professionally

Chapter 9

Writing is the most important part of communication…

✓ Persuasion
✓ The Funnel
✓ 7 Deadly Sins
✓ E-Mail Etiquette

Writing is necessary and important to sustaining your career. Most people just write, forgetting who's on the receiving end: executive producer, club owner, studio owner, etc. and worse, they write like they talk to their peers. Not only does this confuse the reader, but also, in some cases it can upset them.

I have personally placed advertisements asking for specific information when responding back to my company. Most of the time I am in awe at how many people respond back with only a quick, "Get at me," no number or website link left... or, my favorite, the egotistical artist that thinks they are gods gift to music. So many times people fail to read the whole ad or provide the correct information I think I am taking crazy pills some days. I always find it funny after a couple of days go by and these same people, who didn't include all the information requested, write back and ask why I have yet to contact them. My favorite: the Hip-Hop artists writing in Ebonics language, because I have time to deceiver dyslexia and un-comprehensive language with my busy day after all. The downfall, wanting instant gratification without thinking how this comes across as an individual representing their band, self 's, or companies. Or, they don't get the fact that writing so unclear and "ghetto" style is completely out of the realm of reality, and most of us professionals won't put up with it.

To get around this ghetto style, instant gratification, or egotistical attitude we need to learn how to write, and write effectively. Not all of us are naturals at writing and know how to get our point across. Some people really do have problems, and dyslexia, that they should work to overcome. As our quest to become better at our craft and solidify ourselves as professionals, it is imperative we learn and use the proper tools to get us where we need to go. For this to happen we need guidelines, lessons, and examples to help guide this quest in the right direction.

This next section is packed full of useful tools and examples. You will learn the 7 deadly sins of writing, Persuasive Structure, and the Funnel. More importantly I will keep it short and to the point allowing you to use this for the rest of your career without having to read 20 pages just to get one "sin" figured out. I have also provided some examples of writing style to help you get started at trying this out for yourself. In fact this intro you're reading is one of them, Persuasive witting.

While I have given you the most comprehensive tools in professional writing style out there, I have done you even one better, the examples. After reading this section, if you really put 100% effort into it, you will become a great writer and master the craft of persuasive writing. It's all about practice and doing your best while learning from your mistakes. I guarantee by using the examples provided, the easy laid out tools, and your effort, you will land more clients, get more gigs, and represent yourself as a true professional.

Important side notes:

So you've got the band & songs ready and now it's time to start hitting up venues, labels, blogs, social networking sites, etc. But what do you write and how do you make it effective when you only have about 1 sentence to capture your potential audience?

Let's start with the basics. First make sure to do your homework and refer to the correct person using their correct title: Mr., Ms., Miss, etc. Nothing will get your e-mail sent to the trash faster then saying Dear Jon when the booking agent is Adam (you'd be surprised how many people do this). If they have a last name consider using both. Some people like both names when being refereed to and by doing so you have already started to build a relationship with them; it defiantly will not hurt your cause (for instance my name is Zaque Eyn not Zac or Zaq or Zaqueyn, and I am called Zaque Eyn not Zaque or any other version of). Make sure you check the spelling of their name. I cannot stress this enough. If you spell it wrong then don't expect a reply back, although the exception here is if you write a great letter then people can get over the misspelling of their name, usually.

Keep the letter as short as possible and do not add fluff. People want the specifics, fast and short: Your band name, your fan base, how many CD's you sell at shows, how much merch you sell at shows, website (MySpace & Facebook don't count) contact person, phone number. However the exception to this rule is that you do want to be personable and friendly. No body wants an information dump! Put your personality into it. The most important mistake of them all, you fail to mention the date you want for your booking! Tell them what date you want & what time (be specific am or pm counts).

The 7 Deadly Sins of Writing

1. Failure to focus on the business problems and payoffs- the content sounds generic.

You have to think about your audience when you are writing. What is the problem you're trying to solve when communicating with them? Is it the companies lack of marketing efforts or need for another producer because they fired the last one. This is where a little research comes into play before contacting them. By looking into the company and finding out their weak points or problems you want to solve, you will be able to write to them with this understanding.

2. No persuasive structure- the letter is an "information dump"

Make sure you use a persuasive structure when writing to the company. As you will see in the persuasive section of this chapter doing so will make your letter or e-mail extremely effective.

3. No clear differentiation of this band/brand compared to others

Let them know why you differ from other competition. It is also very important not to put down another person or company. However, you must make sure that you not only come across as the expert in your field but that you have uniqueness in your craft.

4. Failure to offer a compelling value proposition.

A value proposition is a short explanation as to how the other person is going to benefit from working with you. This is a promise of value to be delivered, and a belief from the customer of value that will be experienced.

5. Key points are buried- no impact, no highlighting.

Often we get so involved into our own writing style that we forget to highlight important key factors we are trying to express. This could be simple points that are not up front to what the reader wants to know. Think about it like this: When a person asks for how many CD's you have sold in the past year often we don't just flat out say 100. We write for three paragraphs before getting to the point or we write in such a way that the part of selling the 100 CD's is in the middle of a paragraph so the reader has to hunt for the info. If 3 or 4 questions were asked and all the info had to be searched for in your letter or e-mail, then it is almost impossible for the reader to know if you have answered the questions or not. Worse then this, it makes it impossible for them to forward the info over to other people who may also need the info. The person receiving this does not want to re-write your letter or e-mail to shrink it down, and because of this you will simply be looked over and forgotten about.

6. Difficult to read because they're full of jargon, too long, or too technical.

Make sure when writing your letter or e-mail you stay away from slang used in the industry. This would be like saying "When I'm in the studio I use cans instead of speakers." The person on the other end reading this might not know cans means headphones, and you will loose them as a reader. Worse, they could just stop reading and move on. Nobody wants to search the Internet for your meaning of something. Don't forget that some jargon you use may mean different things in different languages and could get you into a lot of trouble. It is best to keep it like you would be talking to someone who knows nothing about your industry so that your information is precise and to the point. Keep it short!

7. Credibility Killers- misspellings, grammar and punctuation errors, use of the wrong client's name, inconsistent formats, and similar mistakes

Ok so this one is pretty self-explanatory. Most people will understand if you make a simple mistake, like not using a comma when you need to. Still, you should proofread everything and run it threw a spell checker and grammar checker first. It's extremely important getting clients names right and using consistent formats. Listen, the fact of the matter is, if you send off a letter, or e-mail, to George and they spell their name Jorge, or if it was really Emily and you got it completely wrong, it is nearly impossible to re-deem yourself. Some people will see this as a sign of being unprofessional and cut communication with you instantly. You might get someone who has to correct you and then move on from it. The take away here is that if you follow this last tip you will save yourself from embarrassment and potentially having to explain yourself.

Structure of Persuasion
--Writing Style--

1. State the Needs or Problems:

The Customers/Venues/Labels/other Needs: understand their needs, issues or problems

Restate the business problem or need (we want to perform Aug. 1st at 8:30pm)

This is the first step in communicating your point, desire to book a gig, work with a company, or any other form of writing in where you want to persuade the reader to work with you. It is very important to know what their needs are in order to express this properly. If you communicate this wrong by confusing the need, or worse, getting the need completely wrong, you will have lost them and most likely they will stop reading.

2. Identify the Positive Outcomes:

Identify the outcomes the client seeks (merch, CDs, fans)

The next crucial step, clearly identify what will happen by solving the problem you have addressed above. If you have identified that the company is lacking new talent to perform at the venue for instance, in this step you give them the outcome of getting new talent. You might say something like, *"Booking a band that has a bigger fan base with a solid track record of great performances will really boost your clubs revenue. By having a band that brings this to the plate will draw attention to your venue as a destination spot for more bands of the same stature."* This is of course a simple statement, but it is designed to get the point across of what the venue is seeking in a solution. Of course it can be hard to always know what the desired outcome is going to be, however, since you are the one selling yourself to them, use your strong points in this step. When giving the solution, it is best to choose outcomes you can provide.

3. Present a Recommendation:

Recommend a solution (we can play here and help your sales)

Tell them how you will solve the problem or how your service provides the right solution. Your PITCH shrunk down into a short paragraph of 4-5 sentences if not shorter in some cases.

4. Provide Details to Substantiate:

Provide substantiating details (past shows or venues)

Let them know why you're the best by providing supporting details. This should be a short paragraph of 4-5 sentences, if not shorter in some cases. Things included could be: past shows, venues you've played at, cd's you've sold, records produced by you, albums engineered, past clients, etc. etc.

The Funnel

Most important:

Introduction: state key point(s)- who, what, when, where, why, how

Secondary points:

Body: present each point in order of importance to the reader

Details:

Conclusion: just stop or, in a longer document provide a quick summary, forecast, and/ or next steps

This style is a finer outline of the persuasion structure. It brings home the order in which you should write your correspondences. Not going in this order, just like in persuasion, could loose the reader, confuse them or simply make them stop reading. It is important to follow both styles extremely well, especially if you're sending off e-mails to obtain work of any kind or land new clients. Mostly, by doing this you are letting the reader know you understand them and know what solutions work. You are also letting them know, in a really defined and short way, why you are the best, and why we should be working together. Not only does this convey your message, but also allows the reader to quickly see what you're trying to get, and allowing them, if they ever need to re-read, exactly where to find the information needed to make a decision.

E-Mail Etiquette

Often a letter can be sent in the form of e-mail, but the e-mail must be professional and use proper etiquette. We need to implement e-mail etiquette rules for the following three reasons:

1. **Professionalism:** By using proper e-mail language, the entertainment professional conveys a professional image.

2. **Efficiency:** E-mails getting to the point are much more effective than poorly worded, drawn out e-mails.

3. **Protection from liability:** Entertainment Professionals awareness of e-mail risks will protect them from costly lawsuits.

* Be concise and to the point

* Answer all questions and preempt further questions

* Use proper spelling, grammar and punctuation

* Make it personal

* Use templates for frequently used responses

* Answer swiftly

* Do not attach unnecessary files

* Use proper structure and layout

* Do not overuse the high-priority option

* Do not write in CAPITALS

* Do not leave out the message thread

* Add disclaimers to your e-mails

* Read the e-mail before you send it

* Do not overuse "reply to all"

* For mailings, use the bcc: field or do a mail merge

* Limit use of abbreviations and emoticons

* Be careful with formatting

* Take care with rich text and HTML messages

* Do not forward chain letters

* Do not ask to recall a message

* Do not copy a message or attachment without permission

* Do not use e-mail to discuss confidential information

* Use meaningful terms for "subject"

* Use active instead of passive sentence structure

* Avoid using URGENT and IMPORTANT

* Avoid long sentences

* Do not send or forward e-mails containing libelous, defamatory, offensive, racist, or obscene remarks

* Do not forward virus hoaxes and chain letters

* Keep your language gender-neutral

* Do not reply to spam

* Use cc: field sparingly

Examples of Writing Styles

Dear Mr./Ms. Vito,

I am sure that, like other record stores, you are constantly looking for ways to increase awareness and revenue. That is why you will want to know more about our artist _____. Our artist, over a 6month period, can help you increase awareness & generate more revenue.

_____ teams up with record stores & promotes them through all of her websites, social networking sites & at live performances. In return the record store stocks her album, _____.

If convenient, I will drop in to talk with you further & play some of her songs to see if the style fits your store on Thursday at 11am. I would greatly appreciate it if you could arrange to have the other decision makers on hand to hear it at the same time. I will phone you Wednesday morning to confirm this appointment. Thank you for your cooperation.

To greater success,

Zaque Eyn

Funksville, U.F.O. -- Creative Empowerment

415.555.5555

Dear _____,

I work with a lot of heavy hitters in the entertainment industry, and one theme rings true throughout, professionalism! Today most people don't even know what professionalism means. We find our e-mails and voicemails cluttered with bands and managers hitting us up with all the wrong information, in inappropriate ways. Like the txt message we never asked for, or the failure to leave us a website when asking us to check out their music, it is no wonder they can't seem to catch a break.

Wouldn't it be nice if we could give people the right tools to succeed in their professional careers and excel at getting responses while building a solid network of professionals?

I have designed a master level seminar teaching the important fundamental tools of surviving, and earning a living in the world of entertainment. Based on my 13 years of experience and education, this seminar goes over: Writing Professionally, 15 Second Pitch, Professional Etiquette/Tools/Skills and Networking Skills.

This 3-hour seminar is built with everyone in mind. From the band leader or producer who does everything, or the manager who needs to boost the clients potential, and even the professional who wants to go further then they ever have before... we teach people how to bring their A Game every time.

I would like to set up a time to talk with your school in regards to hosting this seminar. Currently the seminar is ready to educate our industry with a website going live very soon. I have provided you with a pre-look at the website along with my companies website, as well as my contact information. I will give you a call Wed 11/11/11 at 2pm.

Seminar Site: Company Site:

Direct Contact: 415.555.5555 or e-mail at

Warm Regards,

Zaque Eyn

Hey Club!

We love what you are doing over at _____. I always notice you have the best acts coming in to play and you work hard to put on a great show. I believe it is important to keep this level of performance value rockin at your club.

We are _____. We have over 1,000 followers on Facebook and 200 true fans that go to all of our shows in San Francisco. Each show we play, we sell $1,000 worth of merchandise, and with our new album dropping this month we expect to see that number jump up to $3,000 based on past CD releases.

We limit our shows in San Francisco to about 3 per year to maximize our fan draw and generate positive club awareness. We only work with the best clubs and want yours to host our CD release party. Our band ____ will not only bring in the masses to your club, but will help you to continue bringing in the best the bay has to offer. We also have a great line up of other bands that can fill the two slots before us, ____ and ____. Both combined have a fan draw in San Francisco of 150 fans with merch sales of about $1,000 combined.

We would like to perform on April 4th 2012 at 10pm. We will contact you on Monday at 1pm to talk about details. In the mean time please take a look at our website and listen to our tunes attached in this e-mail.

To the best live shows,

_____ 415.555.5555

websites: (of everyone clearly defined as such)

Professional Pitch

Chapter 10

You only have 15 seconds... go!

✓ Pitch Perfect

Having a great pitch is all about branding your brand while allowing you to get your request for business within a short amount of time. This is an impactful pitch that lasts only 30-60 seconds in time. Any longer then this and you run the risk of losing the intended audience. The reason why this is traditionally called an elevator pitch is because your suppose to think of the time it would take for you to give your pitch if you were riding an elevator up a couple of flights of floors.

While we embark on the journey of writing your own, it is imperative that you not only think of this as if you were ridding in an elevator, but as if it was a bumpy ride at the same time. I say bumpy because in the world of music people have heard everything before, especially if you're in a place like Los Angeles or New York. Most of the executives or entertainment professionals will have more things on their mind then listening to you. The fact of the matter is that in that first initial introduction, the first thing that will most likely pop into their head is "O hear we go again, another person who thinks they are the next Alicia Keys." This means in order for you to be effective you have to fine tune your pitch, and use catch phrases that are unique to your brand. You have to also overcome this, "Here we go again," thought running threw their head, and the only way to do that is to have a hook, just like in music, that will last with them and catch their attention right away!

When your pitch is on point, it will get the other person interested enough where they now have questions or comments for you. Ultimately this is the goal of crafting our pitch and fine-tuning it, the other person is now interested enough they want to talk more.

Once we have the pitch in our bag of tricks we can interchange it with e-mails we send to potential new clients, use it to help us build our mission statement, and even help us fine tune our strategy and direction in the industry, because it forces us to dig deep into ourselves and career.

Essential Elements of a Powerful Pitch

Elevator Pitch/15 Second Pitch

1. Concise: Your pitch should take no longer than 30-60 seconds to say, or read if in an e-mail or on your web-page.

2. Clear: Use language everyone can understand. Don't use fancy words or language only you and your friends understand. This does not come across as making you look smarter and could damage your chances of hooking them into your brand and your pitch. You don't want to loose an opportunity because of this mistake.

3. Powerful: Use words that are powerful and strong. You want to grab their attention!

4. Visual: Use words that paint and create a visual image in your listeners mind. Your message will be more memorable.

5. Tell a Story: The use of a good short story is key in catching their interest, attention, and making them remember you. Finding a solution or facing a tragedy is two examples of how you can craft a story. Use only one style in whatever story you choose as using multiple types will only confuse them. Be careful not to make this to long, keep it short and to the point.

6. Targeted: The use of a pitch is designed to have a specific target audience. However, it is likely that you will come across potential business opportunities for different aspects of your brand. Creating different pitches will allow you to have one geared for each situation you might come across.

7. Goal Oriented: A great pitch is designed with a specific outcome in mind. What will your desired outcome be? For instance: Do you want to gain a new client, record in your dream studio, and get financial backing?

8. Has a Hook: The hook is a phrase or set of words that grabs your listener right away and makes them want to learn more. The use of a great hook will make it impossible for them to walk away from you while making them have no choice but to hear what you have to say.

Crafting Your Killer Elevator Pitch

Write down what you do: Write down what you do several different ways. Do this at least 10-20 different ways. No need to edit this step, just use the free flow of ideas as they come to you. Don't hold back and keep even the silliest of ideas in this step. The goal is to get as many ideas as you can so later you can pick the best of the best.

Write a very short story: This short story should explain what you do. It is ok if this gets long as later you will narrow down key information. Use your words to paint a picture. Have fun with this.

Write down your objective or goal: Do you want to record in your dream studio, gain financial backing, or produce the next big band?

Write 10-20 action statements: These statements or questions are used to spark the action correlating with your goal.

Record yourself: This will help you to see if the timing is within 30-60 seconds and allow you to work out any awkwardness.

Let it sit: Come back to what you have written the next day or later on in the same day.

Highlight the good stuff: Take a listen and read through what you have done. Highlight or circle the phrases that catch your attention and that are clear, powerful, and have visual words. You might still need connector words for some of them as not all the words will or phrases will be concise. Remember ultimately you want them to be as few as possible.

Put the best pieces together: Write down several versions of the new tighter pitch again using your new and improved version. Tell the listener why people should want to do business with you. Include elements of your story if you can fit it into your pitch.

Re-Record: Use the same method as before and record the new ones.

Do a final edit: Cut out as many unnecessary words as you possibly can. Rearrange your words and phrases until it sounds just right. Your goal, remember, is 30-60 seconds.

Dress Rehearsal: Run this by as many people as you can who will listen to you. Use family, friends, colleagues, existing clients you trust ext.

Done for now: Take your final pitch and write it down. Memorize and practice it until it is smooth and roles freely from your lips.

Continue to improve: Over time, always be listening for new phrases or words that you can put into your pitch to improve it and make it more impactful. Test it out. It's always ok to start from scratch because things change like your business or goals.

Example Pitches

Maybe you come across a record store owner and you just happen to have a new CD you're tying to get into stores:

Hi ____ you're the owner of ____ record store? The music industry isn't where it was a few years ago. All the bands are concentrating on singles instead of albums, which in turn hurts the record store. My artist _____ has overcome this by teaming up with record stores & promoting them through all of our web sites, social networking sites & live performances & in return they stock our CD. We've successfully generated a boost in their sales while establishing them as the go to store in their area. We should talk. Here is my number.

Maybe you come across an artist that you've wanted to work with:

Hi artist good to me you. It's so hard to get that analog sound today with all the digital technology out there. I've got this killer Antari tape machine linked up to Endless audio, it's out of this world! I've been producing and engineering for so long I just figured it was time to keep the old school alive with the new. We should link up and get you over to the studio. Here's my card.

Maybe you are sending off a quick blurb to a company for work.

To whom it concerns,

I hear you are looking for a community manager to get social. It's truly a separate job interacting with hundreds of fans every day. This is exactly why I teach, and show, how to be more effective at social communications. I just figured it was time to get social networking back to being social. My resume is included along with my contact info. Lets set up a meeting and discuss working together. Monday at 12 pm is good for me to meet in person. I will call you tomorrow to confirm.

Best Regards,

Name I Role

Phone: 415.555.5555

Professional Bio

Chapter 11

Just a right amount of bragging…

- ✓ Who you are
- ✓ Take inventory
- ✓ One page perfect

Before you begin to write your bio, be sure you have "taken an inventory" of your background, accomplishments, goals, and objectives as a musician, and remember who you are writing the Bio for: A&R Reps at Record Labels, Media Contacts, Booking Agents, Management Contacts, etc. These professionals in the music business are busy individuals, who may deal with dozens of "wanna-be's" every week, so make your bio informative, upbeat, and filled with useful comments, descriptions, quotes, and motivational language that can make them want to listen to your music, and help you on your musical way. When you are ready to rock n' roll, writing the Bio using this outline can keep you focused and organized.

Don't forget that up until this point we have gone over some very useful writing styles and you just got done with your pitch. Use what you have learned so far to help write your bio. In fact I would highly recommend keeping in mind your pitch when you are getting to the bio stage in writing. A lot of the information you came up with can be great for your bio. You may need to tweak it a bit, but it will be useful nonetheless.

The goal of your bio is to get across who you are and what you have accomplished in a short amount of time. I included one of my artist's bios for you to get an idea of what a professional working artist uses. Not all bios are going to look exactly the same, nor will they have the same type of format, sometimes they change. The important thing to remember: follow the initial steps and then tweak from there.

The Paragraphs

1st Paragraph:

Start with an introductory sentence that clearly defines the essential brand/band/artist name, your specific genre of music, where you are from, and a positive quote about your music/skills. Use a contact you have made in the music business or past client to make this relevant. If you don't have a contact in the industry or past clients, go find one or ask a close friend who knows your work. You might not quote the friend but you can use what they say to guide you.

2nd Paragraph:

The immediate purpose of the Bio: What are you doing at this time in your career? Mention a current activity you are involved with or in. If a new CD or digital release is coming out, that should be the main topic of the first sentence of the second paragraph. In other words, a reason why your Bio has been written should be clearly identified early on. Hints about promotional activities that will be happening soon, or already in place to support the CD and digital release, is also useful in this paragraph.

3rd and 4th Paragraph:

This is where you introduce information on any other business partners, band members, background information on the forming of the group, past experience, accomplishments, and recognition issues are addressed. If you have developed a plan for your career path, you can elaborate here to demonstrate how your current project is part of a larger career development plan. Quotes from songs can be useful to highlight your new release.

Ending:

The Bio should not waste words, which equates to the readers time. For a new artist 1 page is perfect to get the job done. For more experienced artists or brands, a page and a half to two pages should be the maximum length. End the Bio in an efficient way; use another quote from an industry contact with clout, or summarize the 2nd paragraph info re-integrating the reader of current activities.

Artist Bio Example

_____ is a freelance vocalist, singer songwriter and recording artist who is known for his versatility of styles and engaging performance. He has sung professionally for the San Francisco Symphony Chorus, the a cappella men's octet, Clerestory, and the Grammy Award Winning, Pacific Boychoir Academy.
_____ has premiered the role of Mr. Bingley in the first operatic rendition of Pride and Prejudice by Kirke Mechem in Davies Symphony Hall, has sung multiple lead roles for the San Francisco Pocket Opera Company and has performed as a solo entertainer for Holland America Cruise Lines.

As a recording artist and songwriter he has recorded three solo albums and has licensed music to shows on MTV, E! and Oxygen networks, such as Keeping Up with the Kardashians, Bad Girls Club, Real World Road Rules and Love Games. He has sung for recording projects such as a jazz/folk fusion in Bolivia (South America) and a New Age Gregorian Chant project in Indiana. He has received radio airplay across the country and even Australia for the novelty song "Santa Has Big Bells" which was featured on Minoan Music's, Music To Kill For Album, and the Youtube performance of "Cloud of You" won him and the band, the Maywinters (Cheyenne, Wyoming), the opportunity to play live at the Bonnaroo Music Festival, in Manchester, TN.

_____ professional career began at the age of 10 traveling the world with the American Boychoir School in Princeton, NJ. He continued his musical studies at the University of Michigan with a B.M. in Vocal Performance. He has toured throughout the United States, Europe, Asia, South America and the Caribbean. He is currently based in Fort Wayne, Indiana and is regularly featured as a singer and soloist for choirs, orchestras, acoustic bands and rock bands both locally and internationally.

Fact Sheet

Chapter 12

Easy access is the name of the game.

✓ Easy layout
✓ Just the facts
✓ All the hot points in one place

The following page is an example of a fact sheet for a band. This may also be used for a producer, an engineer, or any other entertainment professional. Some people prefer to keep it simple and just use the template while others will get more extravagant and make use of colors and other images.

It is important to note who your target audience is when submitting one of these, and may be wise to make it pop if you're an artist sending this out to hundreds of venues, managers or labels. However, it is also important not to go overboard and to get your point across fast and effective... the basic format works extremely well! By adding color and fancy images you may take away from what your intended audience wants to see... just the facts laid out for fast reading. If they have to navigate the page trying to find out how many cd's you sold then you may want to re-think use of color and lots of design work.

Some people will included photos on their fact sheet and provide other information as well. This style would be considered a **one sheet** more than a fact sheet; the main difference being a **one sheet** is like your press kit all in one page and in color with design work implemented. A fact sheet is just the facts, on one page, in black and white.

You'll want to decide what route to go depending on whom you're sending this too. If it's in a press kit, use the fact sheet (simple and basic), if it's something you're sending to a potential client or club and only have one thing you can send, send the **one sheet.** For us producers, engineers and managers the same is true for us.

This should be a guideline to use for anyone, its simple, yet effective and powerful.

Band/Artist Name: Prototype

Musical Style/Genre: Alternative Rock. A mix of contemporary rock sounds mixed in with strong Hip Hop and Funk rhythms

City of Origin: Seattle, Washington

Band member Names and Instruments: _____: Lead Vocals, _____: Lead and Rhythm Guitar, _____: Bass, _____: Drums

Key Points of Interest:

* Currently recording new CD for Fall 08' release

* Previously released two CD EPs

* Sold 500 copies of previous releases at local clubs

* Playing live since 2005 with same original members

* Songs are concerned with political and social issues affecting the youth of today

* Showcased at Winter Music Conference in Las Vegas

Additional Data:

* Appeared on Mutiny Radio in Fall of '07* Northwest tour of alternative clubs and college campuses planned for summer of '08 * Alternative press (Examiner, SF Weekly) has reviewed all previous releases favorably * Interviews and reviews of new CD will be solicited to alternative press and radio

Contact Information:

For more information on the band call or write:

Your Name or Managers Name

www.prototype.com

www.myspace.com/prototype or www.facebook.com/prototype

(206)-398-5445

E-mail: Prototype@prototype.com

The Press Kit and Electronic Press Kit

Chapter 13

Submit something amazing…

✓ Bio
✓ Music
✓ Photos
✓ Videos
✓ Cover Letters

In the music business, the folder that contains your photo, bio, press clippings and demo tape/CD/MP3's, is called your press kit, press package and/or electronic press kit. An EPK is a package in zip file that has everything you have done in the press kit that can be sent via e-mail. In todays age of digital technology it is preferred to send an EPK rather then sending a hard copy. EPK's cut down on paper usage and money you'll spend. Plus chances are everything will be thrown in the trash other then your music, if you're lucky. Pay attention to how they request it, if they want a hard copy send a hard copy. The same package goes to record companies, agents, attorneys and the media. So it should look professional and contain everything you need them to know-- without giving them a book to read.

When putting together your important package, less is more, too much to read will make someone impatient. And realistically, what can you say about a brand new act that has no real career? Your press kit should contain the following materials only:

* Always include a cover letter with every package explaining why you're sending it.

* A clear, crisp 8x10 photo with artist/band name and contact info.

* One or two short, positive reviews or press clips.

* Lyrics to the songs on your tape/CD/MP3's (together in sequence).

* A band/artist fact sheet identifying each member, writer and instrument played by each. No need to mention how long they've been floundering around together doing nothing, unless there's a unique angle to your story.

* Have three or four direct quotes from some very reputable people in the business--managers, producers, artists--include them on a separate quote sheet, but be sure to give them credit correctly.

* Include a professional looking business card from your manager or representative.

* Don't forget to include your demo tape/CD/MP3's

PHOTOS

We need to spend a few minutes talking about the photos you're putting in your press packages. Make sure they really represent you and your brand. Do they show the kind of music you play or music you produce? Do they look professional?

Everybody is somehow capable of finding a photographer to help him or her take professional photos. A great way to get these, if you don't have money, is to hit up your local college. It's up to you to be creative. Make it look great. It's ok to use props such as your instruments, cars, or great back drops. It should look like you've spent thousands of dollars, even though you were on a budget, so the other person will never know.

Make sure you don't do things that will take away from your brand like standing in front of the Grand Canyon so we can't distinguish you from the backdrop. You're the focal point, so use appropriate settings that make you pop, not the backdrop. Don't stand in front of calendars or things with dates on them because it will effectively date your photo. Make sure you don't wear clothes that will make you blend into the backdrop like wearing all black standing in front of black curtains (unless it fits into your strategy somehow).

Look like the music you're playing or style of music you produce or represent. Don't wear rainbow-colored clothes if you're in a Goth band or produce pop music--look dark and dirty, or wear a hip shirt and jeans, like the music. Remember that you want to help your clients, companies, investors, and clubs in identifying you, your style and genre, not confuse them.

COVER LETTERS

As I mentioned earlier, every single press package that goes out must be accompanied by a cover letter explaining why it was sent. Use the tools in this book to guide you.

This letter should be short, to the point, and very professional. It should explain, in a few paragraphs, who you are, why you sent the package and what you expect.

Six short sentences can say it all. Your goal is to get the person listening to your music.

FOLLOWING UP

Sometimes it will take months to hear from these people--even with follow-up calls. Don't give up. Don't get frustrated. Remember that they're getting the same kinds of packages from hundreds of other people around the world, and you're probably not at the top of their list.

Try and make as many connections as possible to the companies you're sending your press kit to. This allows you to submit enough packages with a fair amount of appraisal in return. It will also help you be able to at least find out if the company received it and be able to Asses if the intended person has it.

These packages are your calling cards for your career in the entertainment business. They can be used to solicit a personal manager, agent, publisher, club gig, record label, and recording studios, or just about anyone in the industry.

VIDEOS

The use of videos has become more prevalent in the digital age. If you have a solid video that looks professional, use it. However, I don't think we should only have a video as our only means of a press kit, even the best video's fail to have some important information in them, like the fact sheet and bio. If you are able to get the information across in the video for the fact sheet and bio in a professional way, then I would say use it as your only means. But be forewarned, the company, client, or venue probably still wants to see the press kit, or things associated with it, at one point, so make sure you have it ready for them if they ask.

Professional Life

Chapter 14

You never know who that person is until it's too late.

  ✓ Be Humble
  ✓ Have Humility
✓ Always be on you're A game, always

In this day in age it seems web 2.0 and social networking is taking over. But what about the values we are learning from this technology and how are we interacting with one another? Is typing Happy Birthday on someone's Facebook wall have the same value as calling them?

Recently, I talked to a potential client over the phone needing management. The conversation went well and he did not come across as a know it all or snobish in anyway. At the end of our conversation, which lasted approximately 5 minuets, I expressed to him to e-mail me all his info and what he needed in a manager because I was out running errands and not in the office. He said "I'll txt you" and I told him "do not do that, e-mail is the best way; I can get an overall view of what you need and who you are because it'll have everything I need in one spot (links to websites, music, etc.)." No more then 1 minute later I get a txt from him, just the name and number, no links or anything else and within 24 hours never an e-mail.

Fyi: this was a test to see if he could listen & do what is requested of him before getting into a business relationship together. It's a good judgment of how they are going to take direction and if they will listen to my ideas in the future. Beyond that, it tells me how he is going to treat me as a person, friend & manager.

So what did he do wrong in this situation & why is this detrimental to his career? Let's start with the obvious, he did not listen and ended up doing what he wanted to do anyways. How am I going to be effective in making his life easier and pushing his career to new levels if he can't listen to a simple request? Yes it's true the manager works for the band/brand/artist not the other way around, let's be clear on this. However, it is of the utmost importance when doing business, everyone, including the band, can take and follow directions however small they are. Think about it. If a venue requests an EPK, don't send them a hard copy, they will write you off as a band that can't follow directions.

The other less obvious thing here is what it told me about him as a potential client. It tells me he has power issues and has to be right all the time, again let's be clear, the manager works for the band not the other way around, but it is the managers job to make important decisions based on what is best for their client. You cannot make these decisions if you're dealing with a person who has to always be right and in control: if someone asks you to e-mail them with links, e-mail them with links, do what's asked and nothing less. Simple.

Maybe the number this person called was not a smart phone, or cell phone at all, but the land line instead (it's called call forwarding just in case you've never heard of this new, fancy, technology...): they have no clue; sending a txt to the land line means the receiver will never get it, thereby wasting our time. The receiver may not have the number to call them back in this scenario, so unless the caller is serious (gets a clue), and sends the e-mail, you two may never connect again.

From a business side, wasting energy on people like this is bad for business, so we avoid them like the plague: from the artist side, it sucks, because we never get anywhere, probably don't' realize why, get angry and go create a blog, or YouTube video about why the industry sucks and eventually give up altogether or never quite figure it out; they get one job at a bar once a month and call themselves a gigging musician.

Let's explore one more situation here, the e-mail game. I get several requests from bands wanting to work together. Here is an e-mail copied straight from my e-mail inbox (nothing was change except the band name):

No pay to play bullshit. No American Idol corporate crap... No Motley Metal tattoo-drug lifestyles of those who sold their souls for rock and roll.

Rock with soul. We have invested 6 years of blood, sweat and tears. What, if anything, are you willing to invest?

Thanks,

Band name

Does this sound like a group you would want to work with? Mind you, completely unsolicited by me, no requests were sent to this band for their info; they contacted me all on their own.

Let's analyze this. No web links were provided in the e-mail, which is a big NO. Even if I could get over the cussing and statement of "What, if anything, are you willing to invest," they left me with nothing to check out and see if they are worth my time.

It is very important to leave all your contact info & I don't mean just a MySpace or Facebook link, I mean: Name, band name, website, phone number & e-mail. The person getting your e-mail does not want to Google your band name in hopes of finding some info on you. They want it all laid out for them, if you get 100 e-mails a day from people wanting your help, who would you consider looking at; the person who gave info and links, or the person who makes you have to try and find anything about them at all on the web?

Also note the way this e-mail reads, it sounds kind of rude like I owe them something already, almost as if I should say here's a record contract thank you for allowing me to be your investor... I can only imagine the drama they bring to the plate.

In order to survive in the creative world, we have to take a look at ways creative professionals conduct their lives.

Professional Tips

1. Be humble in your attitude, show some humility.

2. Read and listen carefully to what the other party is saying and asking for: give them that specific info.

3. Don't add extra stuff if they never asked for it (unless relevant in some cases).

4. You are always on "interview" no matter where you are (grocery store, bank, car wash, event, concert etc.) and as soon as you leave the house. If you are rude to someone, pick your nose in public, litter, steal... You are hurting your career. You never know who is watching or who you're talking to. Always be on top of your game, bring your A level, always.

5. Write e-mails professionally as if your life depended on it, because it does. Don't write them from your phone, we can tell you didn't take the time and they look terrible. If you absolutely must write them from your phone, make sure you either are a master of making them look professional, or have rapport already.

6. Give only the important information in your e-mails. We don't care about your bio (unless requested), dog, or last relationship and why you're depressed or have not had a job. We care about easy links to your information, how many true fans you have, how much merch you sell, how many cd's you have sold and why you want to work with us. Keep it short and too the point!

7. Get a real website & keep it updated. MySpace or Facebook is not a website.

8. Texting is not a form of communication. Phone calls are!

9. Rock Stars are Rock Stars because we love people. We don't wake up at 3pm all drugged out hung over. We wake up at 6-7am and get our day started with recording, song writing, business calls, e-mails, meetings, etc., even on show nights. The ones who have longevity & lasting careers are the ones who live this kind of life style, not the party life style.

10. Set daily, monthly & yearly goals for yourself

11. Speak professionally & clearly when leaving messages. Leave your phone number in the beginning of the message... "This is, *name,* 555... 555... 5555... I am calling to set up a time to meet..." If they have to re-listen to the message to get your number, they don't want to listen to a 5-minute message to get to it.

12. Always have your 15 second pitch, business cards, or other fit in your pocket marketing tactic, on you; if possible.

Networking with Digital in Mind

Chapter 15

Do you really think all those people listen to you?

✓ Guide lines
✓ How to network
✓ What the social network means

Most musicians and artists think of only one or two aspects of their career: music and social networking. I find most musicians just go through the motions not really giving it there all, especially when it comes to social networking. In order to improve your skills as a musician, get more gigs and make more money, you have to think outside of the box. Improvisation is a key asset to your bag of tricks and can pay you back ten fold. If you always practice what you know you will never learn anything new, or improve your craft and skill set. Trying new things out and getting out of your comfort zone forces you to expand your mind: the side effect being some potential hit tunes on your hand. More importantly, it will help you expand out from your genre of music, once you get good, and allow you to diversify your income potential by taking on other projects or gigs. This part however is not about making better music or writing hit records, it's about doing simple steps with social networking, like improvisation, that will pay off in the future.

Let's take a look at social networking. Before we get into the finer points, it is important, first, to understand what networking is all about. Networking is defined as "a group of people who exchange information, contacts, and experience for professional or social purposes." Let's add to this and broaden the definition because simply exchanging information, experiences and contacts is not enough to boost your career. Networking should also have some set guidelines that go along with the definition.

We will look at the guidelines on the next page; I wanted to first give you a blurb about how important it is to build relationships. Building relationships is something that takes time and effort on your part. It is up to you to keep your relationships healthy and in tact. We can't expect the other person to do all the work on staying in touch. An important part of this is knowing when and where to pick your battles. If you send off an e-mail, or call, and they do not get back right away, don't hold it against them. Likewise, you should not send them a nasty e-mail if it has been a while or leave a mean voicemail. The other person may be busy, on vacation, or have tons of mixing sessions getting in the way of responding. Don't hound them over and over again if they are not getting back to you, wait a couple of days before trying to contact them again, and if it continues to happen, just let it be, and stop trying. They might not want to talk with you anymore. If you don't hound them or leave a nasty message you will save face, and be out ahead in case they ever do decide to get a hold of you. You never know, it just might end up being worth it when they do.

Guide Lines

1. Set up a File Maker or Address list/book of the people you meet out in the entertainment world.

2. Get yourself a business card holder so you can organize the cards you receive.

3. Build a set of "hot points" to remember where you meet them, i.e.: John Doe - 111 Mina Dance Club 8/15/2009 Musician etc. etc.

4. Never let more then a month go by before you call the person back.

5. Always initiate the first call if they have not already called you, in other words don't wait for them (unless guide line 7 applies).

6. Stay in touch at least every 3 months via phone call or e-mail but don't wait longer then 3 months. If it's an important contact, say someone whom you want to work with soon or in the near future, you want to be in touch at least once every month and a half (1 1/2 months).

7. Don't get their information if you are never going to use it. If they insist on giving their info, except it, and wait for them to call. Unless of course you find a need for them, then call or contact them as soon as you come to this conclusion.

8. Always get back to people within the same business day or 24hours at the latest if they have contacted you via phone or e-mail.

9. Get out of the house and socialize at industry events.

10. Repeat as necessary.

Networking is all about building relationships and nurturing them. It is imperative you go about this the right way.

You should never obtain a connection and instantly start asking for favors or for them to do something for you. This is not networking. In fact, it will cause the connection to stop wanting to know you.

The right way to network is building a relationship and having an open line of communication with your new contact. The professional offers the other person something of value to them before they ever ask a favor or help in return. In fact, a favor or help in return is never the reason why they offer something of value in the first place. The reason they offer something of value is to show the other person they are in the business of building up a solid relationship with them that will last for years to come.

I have a podcast show and use this to offer something of value to the other person when I'm networking. I don't charge for my show and with 1,000 + listeners it is a perfect way for the other person to boost their fan base and gain exposure: a perfect reason why you want to have something in your arsenal of awesome like a blog, podcast, free studio time, tips on better recording techniques or whatever you decide, so you too can offer value.

Most of the time I never ask for something in return, or any kind of help at all from the other person. I only call in a favor when the time is right, which could be a year, maybe even a couple of years, and by this time our relationship is strong and solid, so chances are it would favor both of us at this point.

Now that we have some Guide Lines for networking properly we can talk about social networking. As you may have noticed we didn't talk directly about social networking in the above 10 points. You will be happy to know that these points do speak towards social networking just as much as being out in the real world.

But wait! If I follow these 10 points then my social network would defeat the whole purpose of adding all those "friends." I hate to break it to you but if you're adding all those "friends" whom you have never met and will never talk to, it does defeat the whole purpose of social networking. Let me explain.

For one thing you have the "friend" equation. I use friend in parenthesizes because most people just sit there and add people to their profile never taking the time to know them. So in essence, you are building a fake network of people who don't care about you or even keep up on what you are doing. A "friend" not caring can be proven by going through your friend list and seeing how many of them have interacted with you over the time you added them. Chances are, unless you actually know them and engage them the answer is NEVER. Well if NEVER is happening to you then what is the point of all those people? If they are never engaging or interacting with you does it really matter if you have a 1,000 + people on your friends list if only 200 of them you actually talk to?

"But the record labels won't look at me if I don't have thousands of friends." Seriously! Do you really think the record labels even matter today?

Ok so you're smart, you know that the record labels don't matter but realize that investors want to see results, and fans, amongst other things. It's true they want to see a fan base, but they want to see a real fan base, not a fake one. Trust me, when they start looking into who is interacting with you and who is "liking" your posts on good ole Facebook, or any other social network with appropriate tracking like Twitter and re-tweets, they will realize it's fake.

"Ok, well how do you expect me to possibly keep up with 200 people, let alone thousands of people?" Now that we have our Guide Lines in place we can start to use them in a logical manner. Let's take point number 7, probably the most used and important for social networking, because it states we shouldn't get info if we are never going to use it.

Hopefully you have a brand or band page set up on Facebook or Myspace already, if you don't, do so now.

From here you will notice a few things going on, but most important, that "like" button at the top when people come across your page. Make sure you set up your page so you have a unique URL, and not some generic one. It should look something like www.facebook.com/bandname. With any luck, all your friends and current fans will hit that "like" button.

You will start getting people you don't know liking your page soon: this is a great thing! What you have to realize; they are "liking" your page because they like what you are doing. This doesn't correlate to liking your music, per say, it could be your logo, image, photo's, or even updates.

Never, Never, Never, Ever make ANYONE have to "like" your page in order to listen to the music or see pictures. If I've never heard you before then how could I possible like you? It's backwards thinking and I can't tell you how many times (every time) I've simply just cancelled my inquiry into a band because of this.

The important thing to do: keep your page updated, and interact with new people as much as current fans/friends.

Don't post on their wall "check out our new song (or album)," because you will only be turning them off: no body likes to be spammed for no reason, engage them instead. Tell the new fans thanks, and ask them a personal question, or question, something like, "We luv people who hit our like button. Thnks! We're going to be in your town next week and heard the philly cheese steaks are off the hook. Where should we go for the best one?" Or something like "Thnks for joining our family. We can't decide, movie or painting a blank canvas. What do you think we should do?" After they respond, reply back with something like "awesome that's what we were leaning towards." Then go out and do it. You have to be real, no fake stuff. Take some pictures or a short video, and then post the photo or video the next day: give them a little message saying "good choice! We had a great time." The point here: be real, use your own words, always engage a new fan with something real, and never self promote as your only strategy. Self-promoting should be sparse.

Send them an actual photo or video and you've won them over for life, and you'll have a real conversation going everyone can appreciate. Do this and they will continue to talk with you, and like your posts, which is what you want, interaction. This is how you build your network of true fans.

Always take time and get back to people or, if you are busy because you now have thousands of true fans, at least make sure you do your best. Do something nice for your fans if you are now overwhelmed with thousands of them. Do a free pop up concert in your home town and bake cookies for them, heck maybe even just bake cookies for them and the first 20 people who like your post get sent some of your home made goodness.

Conducting Meetings

Chapter 16

Scheduling makes all the difference

- ✓ Research
- ✓ Schedule
- ✓ Topic points
- ✓ Follow up

Meetings are an important part of what we do in the entertainment industry. I find when you are properly pre-paired, and have the right tools with you, not only do meetings go smooth, but everyone gets more out of them.

The first thing I like to do before any meeting: research the client or company. Research allows me to better understand them, what they represent, and how to talk with them. This doesn't mean treating them inferior, or trying to act superior to them. What it means: allows for understanding of, and insight how to approach, the topics or potential topics of discussion.

Say for instance the meeting is with a music artist that wants me to produce their project. I already know we are going to be talking to each other about specific recording techniques and the way the project will go. But, by doing research I will be able to understand better where they are as an artist.

I never talk with an artist if they have not sent me an EPK, any music they have done, or at the very least, something about them (there is always an exception to what will get me to talk with them; these are just a couple of things I look out for).

Things that get sent to me don't always paint the picture I want to see. If an EPK is done well, I'll have a good idea, but I want to know other things as well. Do they have bad press out on the web or in their geographical location? Do they have as many fans as they say they have? Are they really playing out at venues? Is there anything they have not informed me about? By doing a little extra research I can make better decisions and form better questions when we are in person.

After my research I will have a list of questions compiled. These questions, written down on paper, are taken to the meeting. My list of questions will also include points they want to talk about.

Before I set up a meeting in person I double-check my schedule. It is extremely important to make sure you have plenty of time in your meeting. If the time they want to meet is 12 pm and I have another meeting at 1 pm across town, or down the street, I will try and schedule it for 11 am, or another day. If 12 pm is the only time they can do, I will inform them that I can do that time, however, I have another meeting at 1 pm and may need to cut ours short. After hearing this usually they'll agree to another time.

Another important thing, I make sure to give myself enough time for the meeting depending on the topic. A good rule of thumb, if your meeting is from 12 pm to 1 pm, allow for an extra 30 minutes in your schedule. Things tend to go over, and topics get discussed longer, then you originally planned.

I will also have plenty of blank paper and a writing utensil. Sometimes I will bring a tape recorder, or make sure my phone is charged up, so I can record things, like a vocalist needing help, so I can go back later and re-listen to the singing. Always ask for permission if you do this before you hit record.

The meeting is just a free flow of questions, thoughts and ideas. I make sure to get all the questions I need, and they need, answered. While I am getting questions asked and answered I am taking notes. It's very important to take notes so nothings forgotten, and to follow through on anything I've said I would.

After the meeting I write a follow up e-mail touching base on points discussed, and answer any questions that may have needed to be answered from our conversation as well. Following up gives both of us a record of the conversation, so if months go by, either one of us can revisit the e-mail to get reacquainted, and keeps me present in their mind. The follow up is the professional touch.

Meeting Checklist

1. Do research

2. Make a questions list (yours and theirs)

3. Have topic points to keep it on track

4. Schedule the times correctly and efficiently (at least 30min lead-way)

5. Have a writing utensil and plenty of paper

6. Take notes

7. Bring a recorder, of some kind, depending on the meeting (make sure you have permission before you hit record)

8. Write a follow up e-mail

Industry Checklist

Chapter 17

You can win the biggest show in America, based on music and popularity, and still be unheard of when it's over…

✓ 10/D Rule
✓ Industry Checkliist

The industry is ruff, and the reality of what people look for can be very harsh if you're not pre-paired to deal with it. Fact is, big wigs only care about turning a profit. Of course, they would prefer to have a multiple hit band on their hand rather than just a one hit wonder, but you can only predict so much into the future before the first album, or a single drops. As long as it turns big profits for them and their investors, they are happy. The reality is, if you don't have the full package then you'll simply be looked over for someone else who does.

10/D Rule: Everyone thinks they are a singer, producer, engineer, guitar player, drummer, keyboardist etc. etc. 9 out of 10 of these people will be able to play or sing or produce something, yes, but mediocre at best and a waste of your time. The other 1 out of the 10 will be a little better then the other 9, and maybe worth your efforts (you have to start somewhere), depending on where you are in your career. O out of those 10 will make it in the industry. Therefore a Diamond in the Ruff is to be sought.

Diamond in the Ruff: The illusive talent with the whole package before being discovered by anyone else: An amazing talent with strong business sense.

Aprox: 1-3 new acts a year make an impact in the industry and gain national exposure, to the point of super stardom, and yet those same acts are nowhere to be found in a year or two.

American Who? Ever watch or heard of the show American Idol? I can only think of a couple winners, out of countless seasons, who have actually sustained a career from being on the show. Everyone else is nowhere to be found and certainly not celebrities, or even close to one anymore. They had they're 15 minutes of fame and now the ride is over.

You can win the biggest show in America, based on music and popularity, and still be unheard of when it's over.

Only a select few in the world actually have what it takes to make it to the top and stay on top.

Industry Questions

...In no particular order (except: Do they have a hit? Is #1)

Has the artist or brand in question highlighted their talent the best they can?

Do they have a buzz already and can they continue to generate a buzz?

Are they committed to seeing their career through?

Do they have a large enough fan base (at least a couple thousand true fans)?

Do they have a strong web presence?

Do they have a proven track record?

Are they focused on results and striving towards excellence?

Are they keeping up with current trends?

Are they creating a new trend that's catchy and marketable?

Do they have a fresh marketable image?

Do they have a marketable look?

Do they have a marketable sound?

Will they take direction?

Can we turn anything of theirs into a hit?

Do they have sex appeal?

What is their unique attribute?

Do they have stage presence?

How many albums have they sold in the last quarter?

Do they have any issues? (family holding them back, kids, bills, drug problems, etc.)

Are they good at their instrument or are we going to have to hire session musicians?

What's unique about their playing/voice?

Do they sound too much like any current big seller's on the market?

Should we offer them a contract and shelf them, or try and change their voice/style?

Are they coachable?

Have they ever performed in front of a large crowd on a real stage with a real sound system?

Can they do anything else besides play their instrument/sing? (Can they act, dance, improvise, create drawings, make clothes, etc. etc.).

Are they willing to relocate?

Can they tour 10 months out of the year?

Do they have a good speaking voice?

Are they educated?

What is their "threat level?" Are they going to embarrass us, and the company, and what risks does that pose for us?

How much polishing do they need?

Selecting your team

Chapter 18

Success is a team effort.

✓ Personable
✓ Listening skills
✓ Understanding of the business

When choosing your team, look for two things:

(1) Someone who has the experience and skills to get the job done.
(2) Values similar to your own.

Make a checklist of the qualities and traits important to you:

Accomplishments

Can I get along with them; can relate to me at the point I am in my career

Good listening skills, in the studio, professional environment, and as a person

Ability to collect and organize a large amount of diverse information

Understanding of their job, production and entertainment process

(Foundation to any good team member)

It is important to figure out how much help you will need in your project, and reversely, what is involved in working together.

Is it a producer you need or would an engineer be the right choice? Do you know how the recording process works in a big studio, or studio in general before getting in? Do you need a manager or a booking agent? What kind of marketing do you need?

How to Present Yourself

If we perceive you don't have what it takes to create a hit, or have a budget, the project is likely to be turned away (10/D rule). We want excitement, enthusiasm, and energy from the artist and their music, along with a budget to ensure a solid campaign, as well as, securing payment for services performed. Most importantly we are looking for great songs, talent, and mature people who have what it takes to become a great artist (10/D rule).

Your goal is to get the best producer, engineer, manager, lawyer, etc., you can find given your budget and level of expertise. You are going to have to present a level of credibility, savvy, and know how of the business, as well as, a realistic plan, ideally, already in motion. It is important to be able to communicate your project and have clear goals you are trying to achieve other than: "I just need someone to record me or invest in me."

Team Breakdown

Producer: This is the person who sees your project through from start to finish. They are typically skilled in the art of engineering, have a strong background in music theory, have connections in the industry, and are excellent at time management, budgeting, and selecting the right gear, studio, and session musicians to get the project to a top tier level. The producer also will suggest other instrumentation to help improve the music.

There is a misconception that the producer is someone who makes a beat, typically you'll find this in the Hip-Hop or Rap Genre. This is far from the truth of what a producer does. Making a beat and selling it to someone else is not what a producer does. If the person is clamming to be a producer, but only makes beats, they would be considered a beat maker, not a producer.

It is the producer's job to work with the group, or artist, and help them realize their vision. They are savvy at dealing with big egos and know how to talk and make suggestions that are appropriate for the project without ruining the integrity of the project.

The producer also works with the group or artist to ensure the completed final product is delivered in the best possible quality. This includes, selecting the right studio given the budget provided, helping select the right CD pressing company, helping with design concepts for the album, helping with merch ideas and implementations, some PR work, marketing support, and branding support. Pretty much they have their hands in all aspects of the project, not just a song or songs creation.

The producer will also ensure that the label is represented properly and execute what the label wants accomplished. They are a liaison between the label and the group, or artist, and it's their job to make the label happy. This is typically why the label brings on their own producer and does not let the band use their own, although in some cases the band may use their own producer, but it is far and few between. The label using their own producer ensures the project will be to their standards.

Don't be afraid of producers, or think, they are going to come in and change everything. This is not what the producer set's out to do for you. In fact, they are probably the most important part of your team from a completed amazing project standpoint. They know the in's and out's of what it takes to make a great project come to life, and are going to be more skilled in helping you accomplish a top tier project. They know what works and does not work, and can help improve your music to commercial standards.

Everyone should work with a producer if serious about a music career. Since producers are the most knowledgeable about everything, or have someone on their own team who has a specific talent, they can get way more accomplished for you than anyone else. They have the resources and team to make it happen.

I know everything there is to know about engineering, just ask my engineer.

Different types of producers: Executive producer, producer, music producer

Executive: Has all the money and invests into the project. If they say jump you ask how high and for how long, or they cut your financing and you have to go back to your 9-5 job.

Producer: See's the project, and all it's aspects, through from start to finish, including the creation of music and budgets.

Music Producer: Creates music based on the band or artist's concept. Helps with chord structures, instrumentation, song structure, arranging.

Beat Maker: They work alone and create music for leasing the beat out or selling it to someone.

Engineer: These are the un-sung hero's of our industry. Engineers are the ones who make your albums sound amazing and know everything there is to know about the studio they work in.

People may not realize that the engineer is the one who helps the producer see the band or artist's vision through. They know what microphones work for a given situation, how to get a certain sound, the right signal flow for a given sound, when to keep the take or do a new one, and how much time it usually takes to set up a session. The engineer has an amazing ear and can pick up on distortion, or minor obtrusions in the recording a normal person would never hear. Engineers are the foundation for a great project or song, without a great engineer you won't fully get the most out of your recording sessions.

The engineer and producer work together as one. Sometimes the engineer is the producer, or the producer is also the engineer. This would be typical for smaller budget projects or home studio situations where the to two positions are the same person. When you get to the bigger leagues, then there is almost always a separate entity for both.

Different types of engineers: Live sound engineer, Studio engineer, Tracking engineer, mixing engineer, and mastering engineer.

Live: Mixes live sound for shows at small clubs all the way to huge venues.

Studio: Records music in a studio (multiple roles: tracking, mixing, mastering).

Tracking: The engineer who initially tracks (records) the music. Sends it to the mixing engineer when done.

Mixing: The engineer who takes the tracked music and mix's it to sound amazing. Sends it to the mastering engineer when done.

Mastering: The engineer who puts the polish on the project and get's it to a commercial level, also ensuring every song has the same loudness. They will create fluidness from song to song and handle the arrangement of the albums tracks. Sends it to the label for approval when it's done.

Manager: The manager is responsible for managing the day-to-day operations of the group or artist. They negotiate contracts, put out any "fires," help in the hiring of the rest of your team (booking agent, producer, engineer, etc.), make sure you get paid, organize, and are the voice of the band or artist. They are the initial contact so the band or artist does not have to deal with every little detail allowing them to focus on the music. Managers schedule production meetings with the producer and make sure the band is on time. Other tasks include: time management for the band, making sure the band is clean from drugs, shows up to gigs on time, connects them with other like minded groups, and sets them up with meetings. They also make sure everyone in the group is treated with respect in all situations that may arise.

A manager is not a booking agent! A booking agent is a booking agent. In places like California a manager cannot be a booking agent unless they have a license and are bonded, however, you can be a manager without either of the two. A manager will work with the booking agent and make sure everything is in order for the band, but they do not book shows.

Booking Agent: Someone who finds you work based on what you do –producer, engineer, artist, band, actor, singer etc.- your genre, and what you need to get paid, as well as making sure your rider is in order. If you're solely a music artist they will put together bills (artist line ups) that will generate the most exposure and show turn out; a good one will. They are typically bonded and have a license in areas such as California.

Marketer: Marketing is the process of communicating the value of a product or service to a customer for the purpose of selling said products. In essence the marketer is the one who helps define your marketing plan, comes up with ways to target your audience, and sets in place ways to evaluate the impact of the marketing efforts. Typically the marketing team will work closely with the advertising team to make the most out of your campaign. A marketer is not a promoter.

Advertising: Advertisers often seek to generate increased consumption of their products or services through branding, which involves associating a product name or image with certain qualities in the minds of the customers. They are very savvy at knowing what and where to place your campaign and how to create a good branding effort. Typically they work closely with the marketing team as a cohesive entity

Promoter: Promoters are the ones who do all the legwork. These are the people you see on the street passing out flyers, inviting people to events via social media, and usually have a huge mailing list to generate big crowds. A lot of times clubs will work closely with promoters and create nights around the promoters idea, and since the promoter is the one who gets all the people out to the show, they will typically be the ones who claim "ownership" of the night. Marketing and Advertising teams will work with good promoters to reach a vaster audience and get people motivated to come out.

Interviewing

Set up an initial phone interview:

Who have you worked with?

Can you send any copies or samples of your best work?

What makes you great at what you do?

What are your weaknesses?

What's your favorite music?

Do you have a typical process -production, engineering, manager, etc.- for yourself?

What makes a good mix?

What makes a good band?

What makes a good brand?

Where do you spend most of the marketing budget?

These questions are meant to keep the conversation open to anything. Someone with experience will break them down with good solid answers, where as, an inexperienced person could get frustrated, or try and move on to a different topic. Pay attention, these questions answers are good indicators to how they might handle your questions should you work together and is a good way to judge their character while getting a sense of who they are.

If you like the way the phone interview goes, arrange to get them any pertinent info via their request. Set up a time to have a meeting in person, or if they need to check your info first and have another phone conversation with you, find out when they might call or e-mail you back.

Marketing

Chapter 19

It takes 7 - 14 times of seeing your message before it sinks in…

- ✓ Sticky Factor
- ✓ Marketing Plan
- ✓ Mission Statement
- ✓ Marketing Plan Outline

Marketing plans are essential to your success as an entertainment professional. The marketing plan allows you to think-out what you're trying to accomplish and assess what goals you want to achieve.

By creating a plan, and putting it on paper, you make what you're trying to do real, and believe it or not, will actually get you to your goals a lot faster, as well as, achieve them.

Not everyone is going to build the marketing plan with the same type of products. As a producer or engineer you might say to yourself, "I don't have any products," but that is un-true. Your product is your skills, and it is just as important to plan out how you will market and sell those skills in the same way that it is important to have a pricing strategy for a physical product.

By thinking these facts out, and putting together a marketing plan, you will be able to answer the question of how much you charge, with confidence, when you get asked. Furthermore, it allows you to work out exactly what your services will be. Do you want to just be an engineer? What kind of engineer would that be: Tracking, Mixing, Mastering engineer, etc.? What if you want to be a producer? What type of producer: Pop, Rock, Rap, Hip-Hop, etc.? Will you be a: Music producer, Executive producer, or Engineering producer? What will you charge for each service? How are you going to charge for these services; will you have different pricing structures based on project or hours worked? All these types of questions get answered when you build a solid marketing plan.

Quick Overview: *It takes 7 -14 times of seeing or hearing your message before someone is going to remember it. You have to be diligent in getting your message out there.*

People need to see something a few times before they start to believe you and your message. It's just the law of human nature. Think of all the advertisements on T.V. or on the radio. The first time you see something you don't go right out and buy it, unless the company is already part of your purchasing efforts. For instance, when Apple comes out with a new iPhone you don't need to hear the message 7 - 14 times because chances are you already own one or were planning on buying one, so it's just a simple question of how eager you are to have it right now. Reversely, if you've never heard of a company before you most likely won't be inclined to go right out and get something from them, because in your mind they have not built a brand awareness relationship with you, and taking a risk is not going to be worth it.

So remember when your posting on websites or craigslist, or putting ads in papers, or whatever you're doing to get your message and brand out there, no one is really going to listen to you until they've had time to see your message enough that now they can trust you.

Also remember that nobody likes to be spammed or harassed, so it's important to be clever with getting your message out there in a way that is not annoying. In other words, just because they need to see your message about 7-14 times, does not mean posting the same ad on craigslist every hour, all day, for 7 days. If you did this you will be seen as a joke and a spammer. Spread your messages out over the course of 3 months. Post an ad about every two days, and only post one a day. It takes time to build your reputation, and doesn't happen over night.

Another key rule to marketing; *if you market to everyone then you market to no one.*

Pick your segmentation along with your demographic and stick to it. This does not mean it has to only be 21 year olds... it can be 21 to 35 year olds with an income of $30,000 or more a year, with no family, living in an urban area. The point is, you need to pick your demographic, and by doing so, will allow you to properly target that market, because now you know that 16 year olds, in the example above, won't be included in your promotions. This allows you to target just your market, and make the most impact possible in your efforts. If a16 year olds decide to work with you, great, even better. Think of it this way: You can't market alcohol to 16 year olds and be successful, because they can't buy it, so why bother.

Music is one of those things that can cross all ages, and can be enjoyed by everyone, at any time. However, you must narrow down everyone in the world so you can focus on those that will most enjoy your music. In doing this, it will help you to better build a marketing plan based on your projected demographic, and will allow you to create content that is fun and stands out for them.

By concentrating on only your demographic you can tap into the financial rewards they have to offer. These are the people who want to know your music and you, and would be more inclined to come to all of your shows and buy all your music.

You want people to talk about you in a positive way, enjoy what you do, and spend money on your merch. By targeting the right people you will generate more interest than if you try to talk to everyone. The goal is to build up your core audience, the rest of the people will either catch on or not, but ultimately by building a solid foundation it won't matter if anyone else cares because you now have your true fan base.

Lastly, your target demographic, through their support, will propel you to more of a super star role, because once they start to spread the word about you, other demographics will catch on and become curious.

Integrated Marketing Campaign: Multiple marketing ideas combined together, with a fluid message across all mediums. Instead of just a print add campaign you would also have an Internet campaign, a T.V. campaign, and a radio campaign, working together in unison. The message would be unified across all mediums and have the same look and feel as all the rest. The impact of such a campaign is much more promising, and builds your brand faster, than doing just one thing at a time.

In marketing and branding it is of the utmost importance to have the same message, look, and feel across everything you do. By building a strategy that combines multiple mediums you will be able to reach your target audience, and bring in more clients.

Marketing Orientation

The market concept is a simple and intuitively appealing philosophy that articulates a market orientation. It states that the social and economic justification for a brand's existence is the satisfaction of the clients wants or needs while meeting the brand's objectives. What the brand does or offers is not the primary importance of its success. What the clients are receiving or buying, the perceived value, is what defines the business.

The marketing concept:

--Focusing on the clients or companies wants and needs so that the brand can distinguish its offerings from the competitions.

--Integrating all the brands activities to satisfy the wants of the clients or companies or people.

--Achieving long-term goals for the brand by satisfying clients, companies, or peoples wants while being legally and responsibly at the same time.

The recipe for success is to consistently deliver a unique experience that your competitors cannot match and that satisfies your target client's preferences. This requires a thorough understanding of your clients and distinctive capabilities of your brand that are able to execute your service and deliver the desired experience from your brand's resources.

Market Orientation: a philosophy that assumes that a sale does not depend on aggressive selling but rather on a client's decision to purchase your service. This goes hand and hand with the marketing concept.

Achieving a market orientation involves getting information about your clients, competitors, and the market you are in; examining the information from a complete business perspective; determining how to deliver superior client value; and implementing the appropriate actions to provide value to the clients.

Mission Statement

The foundation of any marketing plan is the professionals mission statement, which answers the question, "What business are we in?" The way a professional defines its business mission profoundly affects the professional's profitability and survival. The mission statement is based on an analysis of benefits sought by present and potential clients, companies, customers, and an analysis based on environmental conditions. The mission statement will set the boundaries for all your subsequent decisions, objectives and strategies.

A mission statement should focus on the market or markets your brand is trying to serve rather than on your skills or services you plan to offer. Otherwise, you run the risk of making your mission statement obsolete as you introduce a new skill or service or take away a service. Business mission statements that are stated too narrowly suffer from marketing myopia – **defining a business in terms of goods and services rather than in terms of the benefits clients and customers seek.** In other words, in this context myopia means narrow, short-term thinking.

On the other hand, mission statements may be stated too broadly. Make sure you get at the root of what your clients will gain from reading your mission. Your clients want to read your mission and know exactly what your company will help them achieve in their career.

The Mission Statement for my company is:

Creative Empowerment: Our mission is to help you reach your full artistic potential, establish your brand, and create a long lasting music career by being the leaders of creativity, innovation and implementation in production/recording, artist development, marketing, branding and biz development.

As you can see we don't talk about specific products or what we get out of it. We talk about services that benefit the client from working with us while letting them know we are on the cutting edge with no pre-packaged services. By informing the reader that it's are mission to help them reach their goals and artistic potential we are telling them we are in this for them, not us. For us, this holds true to our way of working with people. It also allows us to determine what new service we might ad to our line up when we are ready. We wouldn't think of an idea that does not fall into what we hold ourselves to.

By writing the mission statement first you will be able to keep true to your mission in subsequent aspects of the marketing plan.

The Sticky Factor

To make something stick in clients, companies, and peoples minds, we need strategies we can implement: C.A.N, S.U.C.C.E.S.S, Disruptive, and Marketing Propositions. Each of these strategies will help create an outstanding marketing campaign no one will soon forget.

The point of marketing is to spread the word in a way that is memorable, holds true to your mission, and allows people to make informed decisions. However, it's not just about telling a story, or posting all day on Facebook, because no one will really care if there's nothing that connects them to what your marketing. We have to create marketing strategies that will keep the market engaged, as well as, keeping your product or service in their mind next time they need something you offer.

By taking what we have learned so far and applying these techniques in our marketing, we can build a strategy that makes sense and gain more return on our investment.

Creativity: CAN Elements

Connectedness:

Connectedness addresses whether an advertisement, or you, empathy with your target audience's basic needs, and wants, as they relate to making their choice in working with you. An advertisement is said to be connected if it reflects a understanding of the target audience members motivations. For example, if most members of your target are concerned about professional gear and how they are going to get that "radio" sound, then the advertisement that fails to reflect these traits will be unconnected by your audience. In contrast, if you express the type of gear you are using and give them something about your qualifications then you will reflect that these motivations are connected.

Appropriateness:

The element of appropriateness means that an advertisement provides information that is pertinent to the advertised brand relative to other brands in your target category. If you're a producer you might talk about projects that have gone on and made lots of money, or the professional gear you use. You have to make sure you know your strengths and weaknesses in order to use your strengths as an advantage.

Novelty:

Novel ads are unique, fresh, and unexpected. Novelty draws your clients, companies, or fans in by grabbing their attention to your ad so that they can engage in a more effortful information process. This relates to them attempting to comprehend the meaning of the ad brand. Unoriginal ads are unable to break through their competition because it becomes cluttered and unable to grab their attention.

S.U.C.C.E.S.S.

Sticky ads are ads in which your target comprehends the ad's intended message; they are remembered, and can change your target's brand related opinions and behavior. This style is know as SUCCESS, without the extra S, but because it exemplifies success we through in the extra S for the sake of spelling it out completely.

Simplicity:

These sticky ads are simple and profound. It can be said to be simple when it represents your brand's core idea or key positioning statement. This translates into it being stripped to its critical essence and captures the key element that needs to be communicated to your target. These are appropriate and correlate to the CAN elements.

Unexpectedness:

Sticky ads generate interest and curiosity when they differ from your target's expectations. Sticky messages are also creative. Notice how this is similar to the element of novelty in the CAN style. You might use something like a short story that sparks interest. Think of the story of the person who found a razor blade in their burrito. Keep it short if you're using a flyer, but it's ok, for instance, to create a solid 3-4 sentence story on your web page.

Concreteness:

Sticky ideas possess concrete images as compared to abstract representations in their marketing mix. For example, the image of a thief forcing a musician to take off their guitar and hand it over is highly concrete if you are a production studio. Claims about a brand are highly concrete, versus abstract, when they are made perceptible and vivid-- relevant to what you do; produce, engineer, band, manager etc.

Credibility:

Sticky ads are believable. They have a strong sense of authority and provide reasons why they should be thought of as fact. In our example of forcing the musician to hand over their guitar you could be disseminated by attributing it to a publication in your local entertainment guide as a "news" story. Even though it's untrue it will create buzz and excitement. You can post it all over the Internet with something like, "did you see this story?" You could get a blogger to help, or just spread it around the Internet in any fashion that works.

Emotionality:

People care about ideas that generate emotion and tap into their feelings. Our story of the musician taps into fear and people, for a brief moment, before they realize it's a joke. People will be concerned to learn more. The same is true for any other emotion that you might tap into using your skills we have learned above thus far.

Storytelling:

The last element of a sticky ad is storytelling. By definition stories have plots, characters, and settings – all features that are contained in our musician story. Fear is common to many urban legends because it is a particularly profound emotion. But any story that sparks emotion is a story that people will talk about, if it's a good one.

Disruptive Marketing

Disruptive marketing: Disruptive marketing is also known as disruptive technology or disruptive innovation, as in an innovation that helps create a new market and value network. This eventually goes on to disrupt an existing market displacing an earlier technology. This term is used in business and technology literature to describe innovations that improve a product or a service in a way that the market does not expect.

This is a powerful tool you can use to help boost your earning potential. While it would most likely be thought of as a tool for musicians or a band it can also be used as a tool for producers, engineers, managers, and anyone else in the entertainment world. It does not have to be a technology for our industry per say, it can be used to disrupt the way we choose to distribute our music, our EPK's, or even the way we market ourselves. You have to be creative and have a great idea on this one.

The best example of this is Apple. Think of how they changed the market with their iPad, iPhone, and iPod. All these were being done before them, but they came in and changed the game.

Marketing Propositions

Unique Selling Proposition (USP): This was the big thing in the 1970's to the 1980's. It is still very relevant today, however, new generations have spawned newer propositions like, ESP & MSP. This is just what you might think it means, something unique that your competition does not do. This has long been the way we market ourselves. First coming up with something that is unique about your brand. Perhaps this could be a special skill you have, something that your competition does not offer. Hopefully you have been thinking about this throughout the marketing plan process. Once you have determined what your USP is you can start to use this within your marketing efforts. This should be right in line with the rest of your branding efforts, and if you have come up with a killer pitch then chances are your USP is within that pitch. If it's not in your pitch then at this point you should re-think your pitch so that your USP is in it. This is what branding is all about; making a unified array of material that coincides with each other.

Emotional Selling Proposition (ESP): This got started in the 1980's as the way to market to the newer generations. Think of all those commercials that tap into our emotions, this is exactly the style they are using. This goes right along with those stories we just learned about. This is where you tap into the emotions of your clients and fans to make your brand stand out in their minds. You might consider using this if you have created a story that sticks. It is ok to use both ESP and USP within your marketing efforts. Make sure that it makes sense though. Again your marketing is all about creating your brand. Perhaps it's not wise to use both for some, while both can be used for others. Bands and artists are more likely to be able to use both versus a producer, engineer, or manager. Get creative.

Me Selling Proposition (MSP): This is popular in today's time and is mostly recent, around 2000 is when we can start to see this being used more. This is the time we are in now, the me generation. Everything is about me! People want everything personalized, like the engraving on the iPod or the shirts you can order with your own design on them. This is all about options and being able to personalize anything and everything. While the producers, engineers, and managers of the world probably are not going to be selling shirts or mp3 players, bands and artists are exactly what this market is all about. If it can't be personalized then chances are you are missing out on a whole market that is thriving and wants it their way. This is think out side of the box time, and of course the producers, engineers, and managers of the world can use this to their advantage as well. Why have one set price when you can personalize your price around the person you are working for?

Marketing Plan Outline

1. Executive Summary

    a. A high level summary of the marketing plan (written last)

2. Situational Analysis

    a. A brief description of the product/service to be marketed and what type of **marketing orientation** your firm will have.

3. Mission Statement

    a. Answers the question "What business are we in?" Focuses on the market(s) rather than the good or service (written first)

4. Marketing Objectives

    a. A list of marketing objectives that are measurable, realistic, time sensitive and consistent with priorities of the organization (goals)

5. S.W.O.T. Analysis

    a. Strengths (Internal, Things you **CAN** control)

    b. Weaknesses (Internal, Things you **CAN** control)

    c. Opportunities (External, Thing you **CAN'T** control)

    d. Threats (External, Thing you **CAN'T** control)

6. Competitive Advantage

    a. The set of unique features of a company and its products that are perceived by the target market as significant and superior to the competition.

    b. Price, product/service differentiation, niche strategies

7. Consumer Decision Making Process

    a. Factors influencing (Cultural, social, individual, psychological)

    b. Type of decision (routine, limited, extensive)

8. Market Segmentation

a. Segmentation basis (geography, demographics, psychographics, benefits sought, usage rate)

b. Description. What they want. How they use the product/service

c. What is important to them

9. Marketing Mix

Product
The product decisions should consider the product and how they will be leveraged.

i. Brand name, quality, scope of the product line, warranty, packaging, etc.

Price

i. Discuss the pricing strategy, expected volume and decisions for the following pricing variables: List price, discounts, payment terms, leasing options and financing options, etc.

Distribution

i. Decision variables include: Distribution channels, such as direct, retail, distributors & intermediates
ii. Locations
iii. Any logistics regarding transportation, warehousing and order fulfillment

Promotion

i. Advertising, including how much and which media (TV, print, radio, billboards, internet, direct mail, etc.)
ii. Public relations
iii. Promotional programs
iv. Sales force

10. Evaluation and Control

a. A brief description of the ways you plan to measure the success of your marketing strategy. (collect response cards, count phone calls, hits on your website, sales volume, etc.

Sample Marketing Plan

_____ brings your creativity to life. The music and art world badly need a revamp in how it is enjoyed and expressed. The value is being lost due in part to .mp3's, digital cameras and the Internet but mostly due to the disconnected culture of the newer generation.

_____ will have an unmatched approach in re-thinking the meaning, creation and expression of music and art. Music needs to be developed and nurtured so it can be as great as it can. With our personal and commercial recording studios we help the creative process blossom into magic. We help develop your sound and get you at the quality level you deserve. Our _____/events bring the _____
_____
_____. These masterpieces are recorded using video, audio and advanced techniques then delivered to audience for a truly unique very limited edition memory experience.

_____ will use our extensive knowledge of the entertainment industry to quickly gain market share. Profitability will be reached by December of 2011 having completed 3 successful events.

Situation Analysis

_____ will offer superior production and engineer techniques and unique forward thinking outside of the box marketing campaigns, branding strategies, and implementations. All available al a cart and suited specifically to a clients desired end result. We are a market driven company that creates new trends based on our client's vision while creating a demand for new and unique services.

Mission Statement: Creative Empowerment; Our mission is to help you reach your full artistic potential, establish your brand and create a long lasting music career by being the leaders of creativity, innovation and implementation in production/recording, performance, marketing, branding and biz development.

Marketing Objectives

a) By September 2011 we will have 3 unique _____ campaigns running throughout California.
b) By June 12th 2011 Achieve financial goals so we can quite our day jobs and work full time Empowering Creativity.

c) By August 31st 2011 we will have 1 song or album ready to be submitted to the Grammy's through our record label _____.
   d) By November 1st 2011 we have a company EP ready for market.

S.W.O.T.

Strengths

a) Personal recording studio

b) Discounted commercial studio

c) International podcast show

d) Marketing background

e) Music background

f) Producing and engineering background

g) Live event production (planning, booking, scouting, sound, lighting, set up, coordination etc.)

Weaknesses

a) Almost everything is outsourced for events so we have no control over the pricing

b) No venue connections outside of California and Salt Lake City

c) No national T.V. or Movie connections

d) No start up funds for full demonstration party

Opportunities

a) Venues always need good music

b) Popular bands/artists who have not released their new album/artwork

c) No defined green initiative in the entertainment industry

d) A growing market of record labels and recording studios are looking for fresh ideas & partners

Threats

a) 99* mp3 is the new price of the song

b) Pandora, Lastfm, Spotfy, Napster, Rdio, Rhapsody, We7, MOG, and others will continue to grow exponentially in the on demand format while owning your music is becoming less important

c) Talks of albums being reduced to a lower rate of $3.99 to as low as .99 cents

d) Cloud music is starting to gain traction for enjoying music

e) Technology is disconnecting our cultures interaction with one another

Competitive Advantage/Positioning

_____ will position itself as the leader of underground, independent, major: music/artwork creation, along with innovative forward thinking _____ that change how it is _____ _____. We will accomplish this by pushing the boundaries of recorded music while creating unique _____ for client's artistic visions and accomplishments. _____ recognizes that the music/ art industry focuses on one or two key elements instead of all elements pertaining to art and how it is enjoyed and interacted with in real life. We bring to life all of creativities _____for people to enjoy and experience like never before while creating unique opportunities to enjoy and purchase the music outside of traditional ways.

The pricing approach is based on a percentage of marketing/branding campaigns budget, and hourly or daily for recording studio. We have an open relationship with various companies and growing that work with us to offer the best deals possible. Our result is better-budgeted projects that get the product you desire, exposure you need/want with professional precision.

Consumer Decision Making Process

_____ has captured a great deal of information on the industry over the years and has a good grasp on what an artist seeks when realizing their vision. We will use this information to better understand whom we seek, their trends, and how to better communicate with them.

Consumer Needs

_____ is providing the market with an assortment of services designed to bring art alive. Currently most people only think about the recording/creation side of art and the performance with little thought into the design of the space and

_____ people's other _____. They want quality products and events that bring exposure to their craft and generate interest. _____ seeks to fulfill the following benefits that are important to our customers.

Professional Home and Commercial recording studios; Marketing and Branding services; Free continuous support through our podcast show; Promotional CD's; Newsletters, Blogs, and Consulting.

Market Trends

The market for artists is an ever-changing game that has traditionally been the Major Labels arena. The Internet started changing the way we bought music and now it is changing the way we listen to music. Artists are not connecting to the fans as much as they use to by way of live performance and/or when they do play live, they want too high a ticket price, or worse, the show is simply not that great. Fans don't mind spending money on high price ticket costs or $18.99 for albums; if the show rocks and the album has more then two good songs on it, but at the same time, why leave the house or buy the album when they can watch Youtube or listen to the music for free. Social networks connect everyone but at the same time disconnect us from the physical interaction with reality.

Market Segmentation

Our clients our female or male 25 to 55, motivated by self-expression and live in or close to urban culture and major cities. As young or young at heart, enthusiastic, and impulsive consumers, they quickly become enthusiastic about new possibilities but are equally quick to cool. They seek variety and excitement, savoring the new, the offbeat, the risky. They are avid consumers and spend a comparatively high proportion of their income on new gear & instruments, entertainment, and socializing. Their purchases reflect the emphasis they place on having their own unique "tone", doing and hanging with the best, and having "cool" stuff. At the same time our customers are extensive decision makers. They want to know everything about what you can, or your product, can do for them and how that helps their career.

Enthusiastic and Positive attitude towards artwork and it's creation, vision, and realization, our clients seek music production, marketing and live visual experience of their artwork. For them it's all about how they can get people to enjoy their craft, the music, the art. Performing live is as important as is staying creative and working on their craft while having a life outside that craft. They are looking for 2 to 12 shows a month, which combined, support their life. Ideally they would be able to fly in and get to the show, have a hotel to stay in, and get back to their life on a flight out, or simply bop down to their local spot for homegrown innovativeness.

Recording Studios

Home price $250 10hour block or $30 an hour Holiday Discount from 10/15 to 12/31 $200 10hour block

One time 10% finder fee offered for each new referral that becomes a client Includes Sound Engineer with full access to studio equipment:

Gear List: *Mac & Pc *Motu Sound Card *Logic Pro 8 *KRK Monitors *Alesis Hard Disk Recorder *Yamaha Sound Board *Focusright channel strips *Presounus studio channel strips *MPC 1000 *Roland Fantom G6 w/ drum & EP expansion *Alesis Micron *Micro Korg *Planet Phatt *Alesis S4 Quadra Synth *Yamaha TX81Z *Vintage Gibson G-3 Bass *Fender Strat (mexican) *Saxophone *Trumpet *Sure Ksm 34 *B.L.U.E. 8 ball *Sure sm57 *Groove tubes convertible *Sony MDR-V700 Headphones *Mogami Cables*LP Bongos *Gon Bops Tamborine *Clave *Piccllo

Commercial price $550 to $1,800 10hour block No Holiday Discount

One time 10% finder fee offered for each new referral that becomes a client. Includes Producer and Sound Engineer with full access to studio equipment.

Mix analog on a SSL 9064J mixing console and get your project to the level it deserves to be at. Plus the best room designs, microphones, analog and digital signal processing tools to get the best sound possible out of your project suited to your needs!

*****Commercial Studios vary on equipment**

Freelancer price

$__ an hour $__ a consultation

Promotion to Generate Clients Recording Studio(s) & Events

Networking; Client referrals; Facebook and Twitter Updates on Current Projects; Live n Funky podcast show; Targeted Advertising.

Networking: Our main source of generating business. Going out to night clubs, events, shows, art galleries, searching the web for like minded people and contacting them are the best ways to build the company and reach exactly who we want. It takes a personal one on one connection and seeing people to not only understand their art or music, but to build a real relationship. We will make this most effective by having an Electronic Press Kit loaded on our smart phones so at anytime we can show completed projects as well as always having business cards on hand. Follow up is just as important as the initial connection and we will use a 48hour reconnect/call back strategy to keep us fresh in the clients mind.

Client referrals: Key to our promotion of the products and services. This is accomplished by giving outstanding customer service, professionalism and delivering top-notch recordings, events and services. As incentive to our recording clients a 10% finders fee is offered if they recommend our studio to someone and it turns into a paying client.

Facebook and Twitter: We use this medium primarily to keep fans, clients, and friends informed on news, upcoming show dates, fun things we are doing, recording techniques, etc. When it's time for the holiday season we use this to promote our discounts as well. We build up our relationships with our fans by interacting with them and carrying on discussions relevant to their crafts, asking them questions, and answering when they reply.

Podcast show: Our international podcast show has 1,000 listeners and growing, with all types of music. We will leverage this to inform listeners of new and upcoming events, recording sessions, and inform them of our holiday specials. The show is based on exposing the world to fresh and unique art and music. We use the show to expose creativity we work with and will continue doing so for all of our events and clients. This brings what we are doing to an international level and right into the homes, ears, and eyes of people who are already interested and looking for fresh new music.

Flyers in or near relevant places such as: night clubs, music stores, poetry slams, unique stores, etc. to keep us fresh in the minds of people. Our strategy is to promote the show at such places when there is a comparable genre of music or art being performed. In this way we are able to target our audience.

Targeted Advertising: Friendly and Personal exclusive offers. We will use our knowledge of the creative industry to target cutting edge: music, artist, and technology. We will inform them how we make their music "_____." Networking, phone calls, direct mail, e-mail using business cards, flyers and brochures are the mediums we will use.

Evaluation and Control

We will use and keep a contact file system of all the people we come into contact with and make a record of our conversations, their art form, and any other relevant information. We will leverage this information to understand their needs and offer them the right solutions when the time is right for them to start their project. We will use this info to know exactly the right time to touch base with them and keep us fresh in their mind.

We will ask our Facebook and Twitter fans, friends, and clients occasionally what they would like to see more of in our posts or who they might want to see us work with. We will also use them to help us fine tune messages or market for us by asking them to repost our statuses. We can measure if this is effective by seeing who is reposting and talking about us, as well as, using their thoughts and ideas as a way to be more thoughtful to their needs.

We will e-mail all of our clients asking them to take a short survey to be sent back to us. With this information we will be able to better suite their needs in the future. This will also help us determine who will use our services again based on what they say.

Our podcast show is monitored for new subscribers. We know if our promo is working based on how many new subscribers we get within a week of the promo going live. We calculate this by subtracting our average new daily and weekly subscribers from the boost in new daily and weekly subscribers we get during the promotion.

Branding

Chapter 20

The same look, feel, font…

- ✓ Logos
- ✓ Slogan
- ✓ Future
- ✓ Flyers
- ✓ Websites
- ✓ Business Cards

Branding is the foundation of what you are tying to accomplish, to build up your brand so people recognize it, over others, and seek you out. As I mentioned before, people need to see your message 7-14 times before it will sink in, be remembered, and decide to use your product or service over someone else's. We have to make sure our efforts are combined and flow together in unison with all of our marketing: flyers, websites, messages, slogans etc. In essence, this is branding.

In branding it's extremely important to convey the same message over everything you do. Paper, logos, quality of items, and all the other aspects of things people will see, touch, and read, need to have a uniformed look and style about them. This includes using the same font style in all your marketing material: printed items, cd's, albums, shirts, trademark name, or anything else where words are going to be read and seen by the public.

The messages you use are just as important as everything else, and must remain the same on everything you do. You have to break down what you want to be remembered as and come up with catchy phrases that will be remembered. Messages are not just words, but also the perceived meaning behind your design and logo's.

Branding is everything rolled up into one. Everything we have learned so far, in and throughout the rest of this book, is branding at its core.

Logo:

The reason why we all need logo or Avatar, both if you can afford it, is to allow us to brand ourselves with something people will remember and learn to trust. Furthermore, with the use of an Avatar, you can create custom advertisements based around it for the Internet and really step up your game, something that your competition is currently not doing, and this alone is the reason why you need to do it. A manager, producer, or engineer has a really unique opportunity if you are reading this, because this is what trend setting is all about: creating ways to disrupt your market.

For the manager, producer, or engineer you might be thinking, why would I need a logo? The answer is, it puts you in a different category then the rest of the competition. A logo now days, to me, means that it can also be used as your Avatar. The two have traditionally been different entities. The logo is the thing Nike uses, that swoosh symbol, where an Avatar is something that can be animated and have movement for things like videos, movies, commercials, or the Internet. In this day and age, with so many things in the Internet realm, if you had to choose one or the other, it is wise to have an Avatar versus a logo. Your Avatar can be used and interchanged as a logo, but typically the reverse is not true.

Simply put, leaving yourself open to new and unheard of possibilities by making the right choices upfront means you're one step ahead of the game.

Slogan:

The first thing you should do is create a slogan for you're materials. In the music world this is comparable to thinking of yourself as just a musician for the moment, and not the manager, producer, or engineer. The slogan, for musicians, is put on their cd's to let people know in 1 second what they sound like and what to expect, within a reasonable guess (style wise), from the cd. We can use this technique for all of us, and it is really an important factor for our business.

How you construct your slogan:

The slogan allows your prospects to understand what you do, sound like, whom you are, what style you are, and separates you from the competition.

1. Compare yourself to another brand or band

2. Use other names

3. Use famous brands or bands (this is smart)

4. Stick to one thing, don't go over board

Example: Pops like M.J. dusted with that Wall of Sound magic

Does this paint a picture for you? I certainty does for me. I get visions of Michael Jackson dancing and great pop music taken to another level with the wall of sound flair. Also, since pretty much everyone in the world knows both these people, we don't have to think about whom this artist might be talking about, if it were a sticker on a CD for instance. If I used people no one has heard of you'd be asking yourself, pops? Dusted? Wall of sound? Wasn't that Phil Spector? But because I used people we know, we get exactly what pop means, or one of the two meanings (in this case it could stand for both pop music, and dancing, depending on your take), and what Wall of Sound means, without having to think hard. To my point, we also know what to expect when we play the cd.

Your slogan has to be relevant to what you do. You can't use the example above if you were a rap artist because nothing about that slogan says or means anything about rap. If I put in your music and I start to hear rap I am going to toss it, not because I don't like rap, but because I was expecting something completely different.

Once you've created your perfect slogan, show it to a couple of friends and family members, get some opinions. Don't change anything about it just yet either. Your family members and friends could be a little bias, but can be very useful. Write down any suggestions they may have; take notes. After you've talked to them, go ask at least 3 people who have never heard your music, what they envision when they hear your slogan. It will be a good judge if they get your style spot on from the slogan you've constructed. If they have to think about it, or question what you mean, you are probably going to have to re-think your message. Compare what the outsiders thought to what your friends and family thought. If all of them pretty much said the same thing then you know it's good, or time to change it up.

Quality control:

As stated before you want to make sure everything you do has the same message, look and feel. The slogan we have just created is used on everything we do from our websites, flyers, cd's, to even the really short answer to when someone asks us in person, "What do you sound like," then you can drop your slogan on them. Don't use the slogan on one thing, and something completely different, on others. Have one slogan at a time.

Websites, Flyers, CD's, Business Cards, etc.; Look, Feel, Design, Font:

You need to use the same look, feel, design, and font on everything you do. No exceptions, actually the only exception would be e-mail. However, everything else and this included cd's, website(s), shirts, logos, avatars, t-shirts, jackets, hoodies, flyers, handouts, business cards, everything, should have the same look, feel, design, and font. This is what that polished professional look everyone strives for, hint hint!

Everyone starts out somewhere and does not always have lots of start up cash when they get started, especially for this stuff. In an ideal world you would have the funds to make sure every thing has the same look and feel, but "I don't have the money," is the common answer I get. That's ok. As long as you have your goal in mind you can take the proper steps to get to where you want to go. At the start you might have to use a basic look, feel, design and font. That's cool for the start, but ultimately people do want to see more polished branding, so you'd be wise to invest some money into this stuff from the get go. What I really suggest doing is starting off simple in your marketing mix if you don't have unlimited funds. Don't think you have to have everything all at once. Build up your website and get cards, making them your own, as the first step. Pick the look, feel, design, and font that you want, and then branch off from there. When you go to build your EPK you'll then have a foundation to start from that's in line with your brand. Then work on shirts, CD's, etc. etc.

Make sure you don't pick some crazy looking font that nobody can read. Keep it clean, classic and crisp.

Call to Action!:

A call to action is something that drives people to a destination you have told them to go to. This is so important that if you don't do it then the person on the other end will never know what you want them to do. Think about it, if they come across your website and there is nothing on the front page that says "Check out our newest song, click here," they probably are never going to even know you have a new song, let alone listen to it. So we have to always be thinking about what our end game is for our marketing efforts. Do we want them to listen to our song? Do we want them to sign our fan book? Do we want them to give us their e-mail? Do we want them to hire us? Do we want them to buy our song? Tell them to do it! You will boost your average in what you want them to do.

Keep in mind you need to limit your call to action so you don't have twenty of them on your home page. Not only will you confuse and frustrate them, but also they will most likely leave. Pick one and have one goal in mind with your call to action. If you have multiple web pages then it would be ok to have a different call to action in a new section, say you're front page you want them to sign the guest book, but in the music section you want them to buy your album... that's good, just don't put them all on the front page.

Use your call to action on your big promo push or on marketing flyers for your producer or engineer skills.

Future of Branding

While we embark on the branding journey, one thing is certain, we have to think outside the box and concentrate on our brands future. But how do we break the norms? How do we compete with so much clutter?

Branding is more than a 2D experience, especially in the music world. Humans use more than two senses in our everyday life, and so should our branding efforts. It is no longer about simple branding techniques of visual and audio. Think about this for a moment. As humans, do we not see, smell, hear, taste, and touch in our everyday lives?

As music professionals, and bands, we have an edge over ordinary brands such as a tennis shoe company. By nature, our craft is visual and musical, touching on two senses. Shoes have a certain feel about them, and some of us choose shoes based on this. They also have a visual appeal, which sways our buying process of one over the other. Just like shoes, a band already has two key senses built into the product. We have our videos and live shows that promote our sound. A shoe company has to implement countless hours of research and testing to come up with the perfect jingle to tie into their shoe marketing campaign in order to make the perfect, unforgettable sound, we will always associate with them. In doing so, they hope to evoke a feeling every time we here the jingle, in hopes to associate this sound to their brand. If they have done their job right, we will have this jingle stuck in our head and be thinking about those shoes, every time we hear it; a strategy that works tremendously well in increasing overall sales for the company. If the shoe company were able to tap into another sense they would certainly see an increase of even more sales, as well as sticking in people minds that much more.

As music professionals we want our sales to increase and be stuck in people heads all day or all month, do we not? So why is it that every band, or marketing person, in the music industry, only concentrates on two senses given the proven statistics, and studies conducted, in harnessing all of our senses? It's hard to say really, but I think the answer is being scared, not knowing how to, and not wanting to take on what has not been proven in the music industry already. This is such a shame for bands with huge budgets because they are missing a golden opportunity; the opportunity to truly become a household name, even long after the single from the album has dithered away. There have been some bands to date that have employed a scent technique at concerts, but sensory techniques are a truly un-tapped aspect in music as a whole.

If you really want to be remembered long after the album has lost it's mojo, and be a household name, now is the time to start thinking about tapping into this potential. Who says a band has to only be a visual and audio entity? Last time I checked there was no rule saying this is all we could be. I am of course not talking about starting a clothing line here, or making hats to wear; not bad ideas by any means. What I am saying is, tapping into everyone's other senses and making something truly unique about your brand is the future. Perfume, sure, but let's be real here, how many more perfumes do we really need in our lives? The possibilities are quite endless if you open up your mind and expand your normal way of thinking. How come we can't texturize our CD jewel cases? Why can't we create a unique smell that is pumped throughout the whole show: something pleasant, uplifting, memorable, subtle, seductive, and genuine? We can, it's just a matter of doing it, and doing it right.

I don't suggest pumping a scent out in the show that is obtrusive or obnoxious, there is no better way to turn off an audience. But why not come up with a unique scent all to your own, something that is possibly what we smell while at a park on an ordinary day. Something subtle enough not noticed by anyone at the show, but something powerful enough to evoke an emotion. Think about it, if this were to be done right, and no one at the show really noticed it, but they felt this feeling of being outside in a park on a summer day, chances are, when they are out in a park on a summers day, and this scent comes along, they will suddenly be brought right back to that night at the show with all the vivid memories associated with it. This is powerful stuff, really powerful stuff. To evoke these kinds of emotions and memories will not only bring them back to the happy place, the show, they will probably revisit your music that day, start singing their favorite song of yours, and most likely get home and check for any new updates you have or new music they can buy from you.

Of course this type of thing would take some time to work. It's not going to happen after one show, this association, but after a couple of shows, sure. And the more this tactic is used and implemented in everything you do, the more association it will have. Think about it like this, every time you smell fresh popcorn being popped with that buttery flavor, what do you want? What memories do you associate it with? Movies right? And you defiantly want some popcorn when you smell it, don't you? As you read this you're thinking about having some popcorn right now aren't you? You can even smell it, can't you? Try and tell me you wouldn't want this kind of association every time with your music. Like I said, this is powerful stuff, so powerful in fact, that I myself now want some popcorn just talking about it. Yum.

The same is true about all of our senses; we can implement them into our brand or band. Don't think it's possible to taste the music? Don't think our packaging can rival a Tiffany box? Don't think it's possible to touch the music (other than a jewel case that is)? Really? So I guess that song about root beer you just wrote, recorded, and performed could never be associated with root beer lollipops in anyway, now could it?

Remember one key factor in the future of branding, everything must be related to everything else, and must, must, must, be relatable, genuine, and unified. It takes a while for sensory branding to sink in and become associated with your brand, this is not an over the night tactic. You cannot use a different smell every time you play a show, it must be the same one. This type of branding takes years to achieve the association you hope to accomplish with it, an association that is natural and unobtrusive, something people don't even think about, until one day in the park…

Putting together this book

Chapter 21

Elaborations

✓ Phone numbers
✓ Websites
✓ Unique names
✓ Augmented Reality

I wrote this book with one goal in mind, making you successful by being a professional and helping you with your "**IT**" factor. This book would not be complete without key factors that will help you succeed and give you your edge. In this next chapter I thought I would go over elements we should all be thinking about.

It is important to have an open mind when creating you're brand and building a reputable career. You have to look at new technology and implement elements that make sense to you're brand. Likewise, you have to look at old technology and embrace what has worked for people in the past as well as what has not worked for people in the past. By taking a deep look into these things we can start to see how we can shape our brand. But it goes so much further than this when we are talking about your brand. To simply just imitate what other people are doing does not help you out in the grand scheme of things. If everyone just imitated Michael Jackson we would never have gotten to Grunge or Rap. The same is true in building a brand, it's important to understand the competition and use elements of their brand, but you have to make them you're own and think outside the box. Do the extreme, the extraordinary, and be different.

So what are we waiting for? Let's stop talking about it and get to it!

Studio Pre-Pairedness

We have all been there, booking studio time, then when the day comes, we end up working out parts & dealing with issues that should have been taken care of before hand. The clock is ticking in the studio and money is being used that could have been saved or used for what it was intended for... tracking the magic.

Here are some tips to make the most use of your studio time:

You're going into the studio. Practice & Pre-Pair like it.

A. Give yourself 15min to practice each song a day. Don't burn yourself out, it is important to maintain your sanity and stay focused on the song. Two Times through each song is a good goal. Do this each day for 1 week before the session.

B. Ask your engineer & producer what recording techniques they are going to be using in the studio prior to practicing. Polish up and make necessary changes before you get IN the studio. For instance: They want an off tuning method for your guitar... you should be practicing with that sound... no surprises going in, magic coming out.

C. Record your practices with a basic recorder just incase you do something that is amazing. Share it with your engineer or producer as soon as possible so they can make necessary changes if need be or to let you know if it works.

Have pre-production meetings with your team, often. This allows for issues to come up, techniques to be polished appropriately, the right gear & microphones to be rented and/or used along with knowing exactly what is going to happen tracking day.

A. Go over recording schedules so you can time manage yourself for the day. Are drums the first day of recording? How many days recording drums; 1, 2, more? Do you only have 1 hour to nail your guitar part in the studio? Are you trying a couple of different playing styles for each song? Have you rehearsed your vocals? Did you get a vocal coach?, etc.

B. Write out your music and vocals in the proper structure & sheet music for your instrumentation or a chord sheet at least. If the producer and engineer know what is suppose to happen he can guide the session better, ask the rights questions and you'll also be perceived as a professional.

C. Work out tricks & tweaks with your team.

D. Let your producer & engineer navigate the process adding to this list...

Have a clear head

A. Don't forget to sleep! It's important.

B. Chill out on the drugs at least 4 days before the session. Your body will thank you and your music will reward you.

C. Take 20 minutes each day to yourself: Meditate, Sit in quiet; by a tree, at home, listen to ocean waves or nature music etc.

D. Eat at least one healthy meal each day, if not all meals. Stay off the junk food.

Understanding your Web presence:

One of our biggest advantages in today's time is the Internet. Our presence on the web is increasingly more important as traditional means, such as print publications and door-to-door sales are no longer as relevant as they once were.

It is important to have a structured web presence in order to be seen as professionals, and allow potential clients and companies to come into contact with us. We all know a website is important to our career and showing our professional edge, but how do we go about it?

Our website: This should consist of an actual website with your own unique URL. It would look like http://www. mywebpage.com It is important to understand why we have a web page. A web page is something we are in control of. Social networking sites are something another company owns, so when they go under you are left with nothing on the web. I say when, because as times change, so do the worlds view on what is popular at the moment. Remember no space, I mean MySpace? Where are they now? Still around will millions of users, but truth be told, they are pretty much a forgotten entity. Recently Justin Timberlake took a major role in the company, and revamped the website, so it will be interesting to see where they end up in a year or two, the time of this writing is April 2013 for reference sake. The point here is that while sites like Twitter and Facebook are in the forefront of our minds, they too, can end up just like MySpace. With your own website the same thing can never be true, the only exception is if you stop paying your bill or just decide to shut the site down.

Your web page, up until a year ago, I would say needs to have everything that is relevant to your brand. This would include calls to action, calendars, web store selling stuff, bio, music or samples of work, pictures, and videos. It would have a clean look that is easy to comprehend along with easy to navigate features. You would include things like contests, surveys, prizes, special downloads of music, videos and any other information relevant to your brand. This all holds true today, however, with the advent of so many popular web sites like social networking, I find a better use of your web site looks different. This new version of your web site is a catchy looking home page along with your logo and brand name, but instead of all these other features, you have on the bottom of your page: Twitter button, Facebook button and SoundCloud button... these buttons are the companies links to your page on the particular site in question. They are square and have their company's logos on them. This is a trend that is becoming increasingly popular. There is a catch to each of these different methods.

Catch one: If you're a producer, sound engineer, manager, agent or anything else that is not a musician you want to go with a full blown website. It looks extremely professional and puts you in the category of being professional. Not only this, potential clients and companies want to see a good-looking site that has the right information they are seeking out from you. With your own site it's much easier to have things like gear listed with pictures right next it, or a full list of clients with links to their pages, and all the things you'd expect to find on a professional site. It establishes your branding effort, the most important part about why you do this. Think of Apple, their site isn't a Facebook page, if it was would $2,000 for a laptop be worth it, probably not.

Catch two: If you're a musician it is probably better to go with the link style, a catchy front page, and direct people to your social networking site. As long as you have a link to SoundCloud or Band Camp so the person coming across your site can listen and buy your music you will be set. If you are not doing this (links to buy your music) then you have failed as a professional. The other things to include would be Twitter, Facebook or any other site that you use for your band interaction with fans on the Internet. The reason for this is two fold. For one, people want a chance to see who your fans are and how you're interacting with them. Most likely you are doing this via Twitter or Facebook so one way or another people want to see this stuff. It also allows them to see how many potential fans you have. Two, you still own your domain which means you have your own e-mail accounts yourname@brandname.com and if any of these other sites like Twitter were to fail and shut down all you have to do is put up a link to the new hot thing, or you can even change your site to the traditional way as stated above. Either way you are in control still, not the other guy.

Social Networking
Is Social Networking right for you? Think about it; are you a leader or a follower? Just because everyone else is doing it does not mean you should or that you have to. I'm not saying don't use social networking. What I am saying is ask yourself why you need it? If you have a band page on Facebook and never use it or never interact with your fans, it is a waste of space and hurts your branding efforts. If you are going to have these things then you need to use them and interact with people. If someone asks you a question and you never answer back you are missing the whole point on social networking. It's networking after all, not social looking. Be careful with this. Having a page that you never use and only have 5 fans will hurt you a whole lot more then if you don't have one at all. If you have a page with tons of questions or comments that you never respond to, it will hurt you a whole lot more then if you never had a page in the first place.

In our section on networking we talked about how to apply it to social networking. It is important to understand that fan interaction is key to your success in social networking. Asking them questions, sparking conversations, interacting with them, holding contests of what to do that night, are all key components to why you should be using social networking. Likes or followers don't matter, relationships do.

Searching for your brand on the web:

A key factor in creating your web presence is SEO, or Search Engine Optimization. Having your own website is one of the biggest ways people will come across your music. However, having your own website also allows you to tag key words within the site that allow people to come across it during search inquires. Think of it like this, if I am searching for just your band and I know the name of it, of course it will pop up in a Google search. But what if I am searching for a pop band? The chances of me coming across your fan page is next to non-existent. Being able to tag key words is huge, as these key words will allow the search engine to find your site a lot easier when I search for something like pop music.

But even this is not enough to really gain any exposure with SEO. You'll have to hook up with every website you can that's related to your brand, and trade links to each other's sites. You'll have to leave your mark on every blog you write on, every opportunity you get. In fact every opportunity you get to leave your mark you have to do it if you want people to come across your brand through a search about something else, and this does mean even in your social networking posts (but you have to be courteous, smart, and humble, to avoid being a spammer). Don't be a douche bag and a spammer! To fully maximize your efforts: press releases, statements to the press, red carpet events, art and music openings, should be used in combination with everything else.

Unique Names

Another key factor, beyond your web site with key words, is choosing a unique name for your brand. If you have a catchy name like mine, most likely it's all you'll need. But if you're a company, and trying to think of something, you shouldn't use something generic like: Music Company. The best thing to do is a Google search for the name you are thinking to see if any one else is using it, if it is being used than you should come up with a different name.

Once you find a name that works go and get it Trademarked and get your DBA license (doing business as). If you form a sole proprietorship then your DBA should be about $100 a year depending on the city you live in. If you form an LLC instead of a sole proprietor then expect to pay $800 a year. A trademark could run you around $700 and up all said and done, but again it may be cheaper then that depending on how you're filing. It could run more then this and I have heard of it costing upwards of $1,400 so just be aware.

Check your local government office for information on the best place to search for names being used in your area and to find out the specific costs associated with getting your DBA and Trademark.

Blogs: Blogs are a great way to keep up to date with your genre and industry. If your genre does not have one, then this can be a great opportunity to start one. It might just really take off if you put some effort into it. If you're reading random blogs and just posting random comments then you should stop, and re-think your strategy. The first thing you should do is stop reading random blogs, and start reading blogs that are related to your industry or genre. This way when you comment on them you are interacting with your industry.

Stay away from heated conversations and angry comments. I know it happens and you're bound to get into one of these some day, but try and not make this the only time you're commenting. The thing about blogs is that once you leave a comment, when someone searches for your name, these comments will pull up in that search. Brand yourself from the start. Build user names, and profiles that are your brand, so when you do leave a comment it is from your brand (another reason why creating a unique name and trademarking it is so important). Practicing this technique will really help your brand pull up in searches and it's a credibility booster.

Once you've started doing the blog game and interacting with people, when it's time to ask something or post something, people will listen and respect your thoughts and input. For the artist, when your new CD is out and you need a review, the blogger will know your a person they want to promote because of your wisdom you've given over the years. This is why we don't say bad things or get into heated debates we can't win.

Phone:

Get yourself a different phone number then your current one. Yes this means you'll have two phone lines. The nice thing is you can get free ones that ring right to your current one and your clients will be none the wiser. I use Google Voice; it's completely free and allows me to also text for fee. It is easy to set up and allows me to have just a business line. It rings right to my cell phone and allows me to know it's coming from that number so I can answer it as my business. You can set it up to ring to multiple numbers as well, which is useful if you have several employees. Having a business line is a sign of a professional and just plane smart, and allows you to give out the business number instead of your personal number.

Phone Messages:

Make sure your phone message is professional sounding. "You've reached the voicemail box of _____ , please leave us a message with your name, number and the best time to call you back." Something to this effect is perfect. I've heard people burping in their message or leaving extremely long messages. Nobody wants to wait for a minute long message before they can leave theirs, so keep it short and to the point while staying professional.

E-Mail Lists:

It is extremely important in this digital age to have an e-mail list. Since so many of us use e-mail on a regular basis it is not only the perfect way to keep up with your clients and fans but it is perfect for letting them know about cool new things, promos, or important information. The best thing to do is get yourself a program like FileMaker Pro or if you can't afford that use an Excel spread sheet.

I put all my contacts in FileMaker Pro and when I am ready to send something off I can do a mail merge and send e-mails to multiple people with the push of a button. No matter how you build your list, you need one.

Once you've sent off an e-mail, if you're using something like Gmail, you can save this as a group so you can just hit send again from your e-mail. Heck, if you can't afford FileMaker Pro or Excel just use Gmail to keep all your contacts ready at bay.

For us producers, managers, and engineers, chances are we just collect the information as we network. In this case I enter in the info as soon as I get home or the next day, this way it is still fresh in my mind. If you're a band or performing act that is playing out, you need to have yourself an e-mail list people can sign.

The best thing you can do for yourself as a band is to make sure you get some key information. You'll want to get: Name, E-mail address, Geographical location, and Phone number. Most people will at least give you their name and e-mail and not the other stuff. The geographical location you can make a note on your sign up sheet when you get home, or before hand, as to where you're playing that night. You want this so that you can make sure that the next time you're in LA you can send an e-mail to just your LA peeps and not everyone around the country. It doesn't look good if you send off an e-mail and say "Come to our show," when it's in LA and I live in SF. You'll want to make sure you set up different categories for your e-mail files to reflect this, LA peeps, SF peeps, New York peeps, etc.

Keep your e-mail blasts down to a minimum. Don't send stuff every week or two weeks, a month sometimes is too much. Only use this when it is necessary. Your website should be keeping people informed on the daily happenings not your e-mail. You'll also want to have a template that looks good for sending off your e-mails. Use something like Adobe Illustrator so you can make them pop and look professional. You can also use something like MailChimp, that's free up to 500 people, to give you that professional look if you can't afford Adobe Illustrator.

The phone number is great to have so you can txt people when you're in town. Maybe when you get to town you want to do a big lunch with your fans, make it a txt only invite and then it's special, don't put this invite in the e-mail blast. In this way you can explain to people who ask why you want their number, "We do special invites when we get to town with the phone number, you don't have to put it down if you don't want to, we just won't be able to invite you." This is a pretty cool marketing thing and can really build your relationships with your fans. It's also a great way to remind people you have a show that night, or better yet do a pop-up show and only invite the people who gave their numbers. If you're on the road and don't have access for e-mail blasts it's also a great tool for those last minute invites or reminders. But stick to cool promo ideas like these. Don't use the phone and txt strategy with stupid stuff like "How's everyone doing?"

Budgeting:

Most everyone is going to start off with a small budget. That's just the way it is and completely natural. At one point you will start to see money coming in, and then at another point, you will be earning enough to quit your day job. In order to make this happen you have to budget your money wisely. One thing to do is pay off all your bills and loans as soon as possible. Don't take on car payments if you can avoid it, get a clunker if you need to, or move to a city like San Francisco where public transportation is king and cars are not needed. Just don't show up to the A List Party in the clunker, park down the street where know one will see you.

Don't get an apartment that is costly and takes up all your money. Be smart about these things. I live in San Francisco, in the year 2013, and only pay $550 a month (that is not a typo). It is possible to find these things and make them happen if you're smart and resourceful. I don't have car because I don't need one, which means no insurance to pay for, car payment to pay for, and no parking to deal with. I'll rent one for $60 a day or hire an assistant if I need to have a car.

Once money does come in you also want to make sure that you set some aside for rainy days. You have to pre-pair for unplanned things that pop up. Don't get caught off guard and you won't have to go back to a 9-5.

Pay yourself at the same time. I take 80% of revenue and put it aside for bills, re-investments and rainy days. The other 20% I use to have fun with, strictly fun. If 20% is too much of your revenue, set aside 10%. This is mandatory, no exceptions; otherwise you may start to hate what you once loved.

Record Labels:

Record labels are great for one thing, marketing. They get you into the world market, versus just your home market. Lady Gaga would not be as popular without her record labels backing, however, labels are not truly needed in todays market.

I will say that if you want world domination then a label one day might be something you will want to consider, but go into them on your terms. It is entirely doable to earn a hefty living without a label. The money they give you for a recording contract is a loan, that's it. For that loan they own all of your masters and your brand, which means when they decide to dump you, you are left with nothing. Be smart and don't fall into their trap. That 1million dollars they gave you pays for: recording sessions, all your marketing, all your tours, your producer, your A&R, your hotels, your managers hotel, your plane flights, your managers plane flights, everything! All said and done you're lucky if you walk with $14,000 in your pocket that's all yours. Not to mention that you'll never be offered a $1million contract, you'll be lucky if you get $100,000 and that's' if you are a somebody.

You don't see a dime more until your loan is paid back through your album sales. At gold you are just finishing paying them back, so unless you sell more then gold and get to platinum, chances are you'll never make any more then that $14,000.

Labels will get you into the global market though, so is it really worth it? I don't think it is, and recommend you don't do it unless you're already gaining so much traction, and exposed, you hold all the power over them. Should that day arise, I feel the conversation of signing can happen.

Honestly you are better off getting money from other means while still holding the rights to your music. A famous band I work with got paid close to $50,000 and received a car for doing a car commercial. They also were so good at what they do they told the car company that if they were going to do the commercial they had to produce and film it themselves because that is the only way they could get the chemistry they have on film... the car company said how many cameras do you want us to send you? True story, and I have never in my life heard this kind of pull from a band, not even the Rolling Stones get this kind of treatment. That money and car they got, all theirs. No rights to their music were given up or anything owed back to the car company. One day they may decide to except a labels offer, they've had 2 majors hit them up, but they already have their own negotiating power to call shots and how they want things done. They also make over $100,000 a year through song sales, which is more then the signed artist with a 1million dollar contract.

If you're a producer then your work is cut out for you with record labels. It use to be you would get a good chunk of change up front and points on the back end to produce a song. Now days because technology is vast and anyone can produce a song, labels expect more from us. Unless you are a top tier producer with a lot of credits on your record then you are more likely to be asked to give them a final product before any pay is to happen. This means that you will need access to a commercial quality studio to produce the project before they give you anything.

If you're starting out and you get a label interested in you this could mean a lot of money out of your pocket up front. So be careful and know what you're getting yourself into. If you don't have a hook up at a studio or can get commercial quality product from your personal studio then you have to ask yourself, is the cost worth your time? If it's going to cost you $5,000 to produce one song you're going to have to weigh how much this could really help your career. I'm not saying don't do it, I am saying be smart about it. The best thing you can do for yourself in the early part of your career is build a network up of good commercial studios that you can use for free or at a good discount should the right situation present itself.

Changing the Game:

How do you change the game? One thing is certain, you have to think outside the box. Network the right way and get programmers, studios, engineers, producers, managers, and the like in and on your team. This will help you out with future ideas.

Dig deep in your industry. What is not happening with technology that can happen? Pretty much anything is possible now days.

Augmented reality: Can you use this technology to start a trend? I think you can. With the majority of people using smart phones and iPads it is a great time to implement this technology and use it towards your advantage. Got a hot pop signer that exudes sexy? Does she love flaunting it on stage? Why not take this technology a step further and create an augmented reality show? You could set up the technology to make it appear as if she were wearing a bikini on stage while she sang, even though she was fully clothed. Or maybe all those posters you have of her could show off her new underwear line when the technology is used, but show her in a swag outfit when it's not being used. A little over the top? Sure it is, but that's the point! How fast would your posters sell if I could see that sexy girl in her underwear line using a smart phone and this technology... pretty dam fast! And what a way to promote her new underwear line, it would be the coolest secret that went viral over night. The buzz alone would be worth it, not to mention the sales of posters and the underwear.

Avatar: If you've created an avatar why not use it to take the world by storm? You could create an animated cartoon and show off you producing or engineering the new song you're working on, maybe a virtual lesson of sorts. Or maybe, just maybe, use technology like it's never been used before. How cool would it be to have an avatar that popped up on your computer and danced when iTunes was playing? You could create a program that works seamlessly with iTunes and have the avatar not only dance when music is played but guide you through song selections and help you pick new songs. You could even have the avatar be the new search feature on the computer. Simply install the program and let the avatar help you with everything. Think Microsoft paper clip guy on some serious crack. Extreme? Yes! But I guarantee you that with the right programmer and some very creative thought into this, you would never have to worry about money again. Every music artist in the world would want his or her own avatar to do this. You would have to create a whole company just to make this possible for everyone.

Games: Everyone loves a great game. Use a game to create awareness of your brand. Make it a treasure hunt to your studio, or website, or concert. Implement augmented reality into it. Do something crazy like shower your city with posters with a tag line like "Michael Jackson Lives," with a QR Code. When they use the QR Code it takes them right to a website that starts the hunt around the city. Maybe the first spot is a local music store where they get a discount for finding it. Then they get another QR Code that leads them to your favorite inspiration spot where they get another QR Code that then leads them right to your concert the next day. Of course you would have at one point instructed them what the end game was so they knew what they were playing. You can really get creative with a game, and although my example is really basic, you get the idea. By including that local store perhaps you have worked out a deal with them where they always put your music in the best purchasing spot... like right next to the hot artist of the moment.

Apps: Smart phone apps are so popular you can tap into this technology and make it work for you. Maybe create a producer tips app that helps up and coming producers. Or create an engineering app that lets you see what the pros do in a given situation. Maybe make that avatar work for you and have it spouting off funny studio stories. What is the industry not doing you're doing? Make an app for that. But don't just make one because it's what so many people are doing right now. You have to approach it smart, and make it really unique, powerful, and useful.

Music Packaging: Who says your music has to be packaged in a regular jewel case? Get creative in how you present your media. One album I worked on was a homegrown style that was all about do it yourself and simplistic. We were walking one day and came across old kids stories that looked like mini albums. They were tough paper and very durable, each with a unique story. Something from the 70's I think. At the time we didn't know what to do with them but considering there was about 300 of them we grabbed them and took them back to the studio. One of the stories we turned into a song, funny as it sounds, but it turned out fantastic. Of the 300 stories, each one had about 20 of each, so all in total we had about 15 different stories. We ended up turning these into the album cover and placed the cd inside. These were original and unique, but also they were one of a kind; all the more reason for people to buy them. You could do the same thing. Does your music or your style have a lot to do with art? Perhaps you could create artwork that is playable. Make the artwork viewable with augmented reality and when someone looks at it with his or her smart phone it sends him or her on a journey that is your music. Think outside the box and give people a reason to buy your music other then your talent. Make them unique and different, original and one of a kind. Or just do the unimaginable.

?: Did I get your mind working? Game changing is all about thinking outside the box and doing the unthinkable. Every one of us has an idea that could really be useful and powerful to other people. It's the successful ones who actually do it and make it happen. But you have to keep it relevant to your profession in order to make it work for you. This may not always be the case, but trust me, if you're not an event promoter and you try and make a game that leads people to your recording studio it probably is not going to work to your advantage.

As the entertainment industry has lost their grip on album sales it has had an effect on how we need to approach our profession. Technology is out there that is not being used in the right way or not being used at all. It takes someone like you to change the game and create a new market for music and your craft. Don't be a follower, be a leader. The producer might think it's funny to build an avatar let alone create a program around it that helps people out. At the same time, if you're the one doing this, you would have single handily changed the game forever. What you have to remember is there are thousands of artists, producers, engineers, and managers that all want a piece of the action. With technology in everyone's hands and able to create a quality song, what makes you different? Who cares if you've worked with so and so, what are you doing now? Anybody can be an artist, producer, engineer, or manager today. If you are going to create a lasting career you need to diversify and create avenues that no one else is doing to separate you from the masses. The only way to do this is to continually work on your craft and lead a professional life while doing the unthinkable.

The Future

Chapter 22

Looking ahead into what was once unknown.

✓ Social 2.0
✓ What the new web looks like.
✓ What the future of the industry is.

What about a hybrid website and Web 3.0? When you have so many platforms to get your brand out there how do you choose, accomplish, achieve and succeed? The answer is finding your strong points and tightening the loose ones while creatively diversifying resources to yours and their advantage. A hybrid website and other technologies coming together and being integrated into real life is known as Web 3.0 and Social 2.0.

We live in a time when thinking outside the box and doing the extreme and daring is what propels us into the success category. To get to the success category we must use all of our resources and tap into our vast network. It is important to utilize all the technology your tribe has at its disposal when branching out into the real world. Let us apply this to our campaign and website.

The hybrid website, Web 3.0, and Social 2.0 have elements; music, art, fashion, visual and full sensory experience bridging all these things together; *everything creative has elements of everything else creative in it*. The website can be our vehicle to a means taken in a whole new direction. The new trend in web 3.0 will implement Augmented Reality and similar technologies into them in new and forward thinking ways allowing people to interact with the brand and one another in real life. This will allow a user to have an app that can be used on their phone to get engaged with the brand in a whole new way. When the app is pointed at the web site, it comes to life. To the right you have a free song download at www.freesongdownload.com (made up site), to the left is a link to a special video at a www.specialvideo.com (made up site), and in the center you have a visual experience that goes along with your brand, a special trailer for your brand that is a cartoon or perhaps an organic visual that brings to life the picture. On the bottom you have a link that informs you of all the news about the brand and upcoming shows while the top hosts the link for a mobile site. The mobile site, upon opening, tells you how to find the non-augmented reality site on the web as well as letting you explore the mobile site's content of interactive music, art, fashion and other elements. The mobile site will allow seamless integration into real world versions of what you see on the site. A choose your own adventure song/video experience, full of animation and geographical location enhancement that also helps change the experience based on where you are in a given city, will further the experience when the mobile site is implemented with Augmented Reality. To further the experience when you're at these geographical locations your marketing flyers/artwork at these locations will have added augmented reality built in so if you use the app to look at those you get more exclusive content. The clothing you sell also has augmented reality built in so anyone wearing the clothing becomes a part of the experience. Using the app to look at the clothing you can see another exclusive video short, or secret messages that ties into the campaign.

This is a hybrid version at its basic form and what Web 3.0 is all about—full integration of mobile, iPad, home based computing (desk top, laptop), and real life. Believe it or not, this is where all the new technology is going to be taking us. It no longer will be about a website, basic or full of content, it will be about added value that uses technology in new ways. Websites are old and outdated as well as apps that only give you a one sided experience. The hybrid version is the future of the technology we have created—web, mobile phones and computers—and how we will use them going forward.

Future of the Music Industry

No doubt we are in an era of changing times. Traditional radio is no longer making or breaking artists, record labels are no longer breaking artists as once ago, and the Internet has saturated the market with thousands of new bands popping up almost every couple of months because of cheaper access to recording equipment.

So what lies ahead in the music industry, what does the future hold for us? To answer this, is a question that, well, can never truly be answered with any certainty. We see a trend to get our music on Pandora, and Spotify, only to bash them for not paying artist what they are worth, even though traditional radio never paid the artist anything for playing their music. We see music services pop up on the Internet just as fast as others are shutting their doors. It is a time of confusion, and a time of empowerment, like we have never before seen in the music industry.

The truth is the same as it has always been, making great music and having velocity. Sure, anyone can record anything, on any budget, and push out music daily. We can get our music in the eyes and ears of thousands, if not millions, of people with the click of a button or two, in the matter of seconds. What we don't see is true development, of any kind, like we use to. It's more important to get as many likes and followers as possible so we can hound them with constant buy me, listen to me, re-post this, re-post that, than it is to build real relationships. And all of this because, like with anything new, we are excited about new technology that gives us the power, not "them" the power.

Sometimes we have to take a step back: listen, look, and learn before we jump in. The downfall of the Internet is there isn't a roadmap; everyone has access to sports cars with lanes going 100mph, and more, with no cops in sight. No one takes time to stop and ask for directions, they just put the petal to the metal and burn rubber.

Even just a few years back it was impossible to send an e-mail with an .aiff file attachment because e-mail couldn't handle big files, we needed something like YouSendIt to get the job done for us. Then came the Cloud, a way for storing our info in the inter-webs, forever, without ever having to use a hard drive again. Technology moves at such a fast past in todays era it's hard to believe 20 years ago cell phones were just coming out.

The future of the music industry will always be something revolutionary in the way of new technology. Something that makes our lives easier will always be tweaked to the point it works brilliantly within the music industry. It's just a fact.

The future of the music industry for brands and artists, however, will be the change in how we perceive these technologies and use them to our advantage. It will be the engineer who comes up with a software program that allows us to make a live Avitar on our computer screen for the world to use and interact with. It will be the artist who comes up with a new instrument using technologies put to the side by big companies like Google. It will be the person who figures out how to brain map our minds with a helmet to express our musical thoughts, B.T. is already working on something like this and hopefully one day it becomes a reality.

The more immediate future of our industry, however, is not so far off. One thing we will see is the use of companies like Scion investing into artists with nice chunks of money in exchange for a commercial. A win-win for the artist because not only do they get exposure, they get money which is <u>not a loan</u> like with record label advances. This is, of course not entirely new, but we will start to see a lot more of it, especially once artists figure this out and start to write music geared towards these companies.

We will also start to see more cross branding, primarily with more popular artists, working deals with companies to include their music with the a product. Expect to see more deals with music being included with car purchases or getting an exclusive album when you buy a plan ticket on Virgin Airlines. Again reserved for popular artists, but we will see more of these trends happing sooner that later. And why wouldn't we, if it adds value to the brand and the artist get's their album out in a unique co-branding opportunity, it makes perfect sense. I want an album to listen to when I fly form San Francisco to New York, how cool is that!

When we see up swings in technology advancing, at the pace it does, we can expect to see old trends making a come back as well. If you want to look into the future, look into the past. In the next few years we may start to see a slight comeback of the cassette tape. Why? Because people who are smart collect things they don't need then sell them at swap meets or garage sales only for someone like you to come across these gems and exploit them. We will see some bands finding huge supplies of old, perfect, portable cassette players and harnessing their power. Why not buy up those hundred portable cassette players and then make a limited edition tape to go along with it? This of course brings me to the main point of this comeback topic. The do-it-yourselfer.

We will see a trend in the DIY arena of really cool things happening over the next three years or so. This will be of the hacker type mentality. A bunch of old cell phones left for dead, turned it into a music player for your album? It can be done with the right person programing it. If it's old, outdated, and can be repurposed there is a market for it, if it's cool enough and not too cheesy.

But this new DIY'er mentality will flourish beyond just hacking something old and repurposing it. We will see albums people can actually play, instead of simply listening to them. It's been done before, but has yet to be fully tapped into, because for so long the major labels have been scared to embrace anything new beyond what they already know. As we see more computer and electrical engineers tapping into their creative side, we will see more unique music listening opportunities. Things like playable CD cases, or playable posters, and even video flyers that show your music video in full. This is the DIY music hacker, and we will see them flourish in the years to come.

It will go beyond being able to play the album, or create your own music with their included creations as well. The DIY music hacker will create new ways of listing to, and experiencing music, entirely. They will start to create and improve upon things like earth boxes. Earth boxes, will be something in the realm of music devices harnessing the power of the earth. For instance, when an earth box is placed outside and the wind blows over it, it will start to play a song from their, or your, album, in public, all on it's own with no batteries required. This is not a fantasy I am speaking of, it's already a reality; one we will start to experience more of very soon. And once we experience something like this for ourselves, its mesmerizing, hypnotic architecture will still our ears for years to come. The expression will no longer just be stop and smell the roses, it will be stop and enjoy the music.

Remember those days of yester year when you had to go to 3 check points, or call 1 hour before, to find the party. And when you got there it was at a secret location, not some club claiming to be a secret location? Bands and DJ's alike are going to start tapping back into this mentality and creating unique underground events. Being these are underground, the chances of the average person finding out about them will be slim, could be slim. But it isn't going to just be of the underground variety, because when popular bands start to tap into this it is impossible to hide the buzz it will generate. More and more bands will be using this to help generate community and bring back some of the underground flair. Expect bands and DJ's to start putting on more secret location parties, parties that are for the dedicated fans, the fans who put their ear to the social media ground, and listen for fun and exciting things from their favorite groups. After all, who doesn't love a great secret party at secret locations?

The rejuvenated party craze will bring with it, fun new ways for fans to enjoy experiences. Bands are starting to wise up to building community and connecting with fans, rather than only caring about fattening their pocket book. Because of this new commitment to their fans, we are going to start to see more things like home made cookie parties, album artwork parties, music video parties… think of it as the new crowd funding. Whereas the old crowd funding was all about asking fans for money to support their projects, cool but outdated, the new crowd funding is all about asking fans to be involved in projects, and really building a community.

Egos

Chapter 23

It's not what you thought it was.

✓ The real ego
✓ Why famous people get a bad wrap

We think of big egos as generally being "all about me," or attitude of being better than everyone else, perhaps even rude, however, this is not always the case. A big ego expects things to be carried out with precision and without question to their authority; they want greatness at all times. In the music industry we are going to come across very big egos, therefore, we need an understanding in order to work and deal with them.

The time I worked with, we'll call her Ms. Cook, is a great example of our perceived perception of big egos and why being mean or rude does not correlate; it is only a perception, not the reality we tend to think.

I personally enjoyed working with Ms. Cook, but my experience was different from the other person in this story because I understand big personalities, while the other person did not.

Having worked with big personalities, I mentally pre-paired myself for the day with Ms. Cook, as I always do before working with anyone, to boost my energy and release any stress in my body so I can give 100% and stay focused. My strategy is pre-pairing for the worse case scenario so mentally and physically I am ready to handle anything they might throw my way.

When someone has been in the game for as long as she has, they become to expect and demand professionalism at all times, and if you're not mentally pre-paired, their ego will drain your energy and leave you crying in the corner before you know it, I've seen it happen. Being catered to at all times, and with the snap of a finger a full crew jumping to make it happen, it becomes expected you do and act the same because they are accustom to it. Giving 99-100% all the time, they expect people around them to do the same, and do not want slackers or those who cannot follow directions around them.

As I worked setting up the backstage, and making sure everything was running smoothly for her, she came up to me and asked if the catering company brought any soup. Instead of blurting out a yes or no answer, or saying I didn't know, I said, "I am not sure Ms. Cook, but let me know what kind you like and I will make it happen." She expressed it was ok if they didn't have any, but I wasn't going to let her go without soup, so I gave some encouraging words and let her know I would have it in 30 minutes. Of course the caterers didn't have any soup, it was a mad dash, but I made it happen and within the time frame I said I would because I knew, even if they didn't have any soup, I was close enough to plenty of places I could grab some for her. For all I know it could be a ritual, and who am I to question it, or frustrate her with arbitrary comments or questions; just make it happen if it's realistic.

I became know as the soup guy and a hero in her eyes by the end of the day, and not because of the soup or the fact I was helping run the back stage, but because I treated her with respect, held true to my word, and understood how important it was for her to have what she needed. Take this into contrast our monitor engineer who got fired after this same day.

Ms. Cook is old school, and likes a certain sound, so performing with analog mixing gear is the only way to achieve this sound; a lost art in todays digital world.

Using analog gear for live performance posses certain issues, just like it's digital counterpart. Feedback from stage monitors is one such issue when using analog. Digital technology typically provides more control over feedback because we have more tools at our disposal to counteract it, or stop it before it ever happens, whereas in analog, we are limited to the gear we brought. For instance, if we didn't bring additional EQ's to help us, it becomes a little harder to handle feedback on the fly, or conversely, we brought to many and now there is too much to tweak on the fly.

Since she likes old school sound, and the only way to get this is with specific analog gear, the monitor engineer, apparently, was not as familiar with the inherent issues associated with it. The way the stage was set up, and Ms. Cook's mandatory request of a bump in the 10k range, meant we were destine to have feedback issues. Requests for a bump, in any frequency range, is a double edge sword in engineer land if you have not had a proper sound check, because you don't know where you're feedback frequency's are going to be. If you have had a proper sound check, as we did this day, there should never be any issue that can't be fixed on the fly. As an engineer, we can only do so much provided what tools we have at our disposal, but regardless, it's still our job to make sure things run smoothly. Experience is our biggest tool and if you don't have as much of it, it can be difficult to correct issues on the fly, especially when it's not your typical set up.

What separates the person who gets continued work, versus someone who gets fired, is how a given situation is handled. The obvious way to handle a feedback issue is to cut the frequency giving you the problem, but if that frequency is the one the artist told you to turn up what do you do? And what do you do when the artist keeps telling you to turn up the monitors, but is obviously not pleased with the feedback?

I could write a whole book on engineering tricks, and some day maybe I will, but for the sake of this book I won't get into tricks to correct the feedback issue. I will however tell you what you don't do in this situation. You don't continually tell the artist "This isn't what I normally do, I'm not a monitor engineer, I don't mix live shows." And you most certainly don't do this with attitude throughout the show you were hired on to mix. The engineer in question did exactly this. Talk about shooting yourself and career, in the foot.

The look on Ms. Cook's face was of shock and disgust: you could feel her anger when the engineer said these things, and mind you it was said a good 8 times, heightening the frustration for everyone, throughout the show. The feedback lasted throughout the entire show, after it started in the second song, but Ms. Cook kept performing like a champ, never stopping the show or walking off stage.

Could the request for a bump in the 10k frequency have been a trick to make sure she got a proper sound check for herself? I doubt it. Why would she sabotage her own show; seems highly unlikely. It also is highly unlikely she was trying to be egotistical and spiteful to the engineer, or anyone working the show, again why would she sabotage her own show? It would seem more likely the engineer tried to sabotage the show, but feedback is not something pleasant to listen to, so it's unlikely the engineer tried anything fishy.

Although, the engineer certainly did nothing to try and improve the situation by either cutting the problem frequency, or ride the frequency so Ms. Cook could have had her bump without the feedback, they shut down and made the situation worse by basically letting everyone know she didn't care.

To this day, it is still beyond me why the engineer would try and take the blame off in such a way as to frustrate everyone, including the artist, while putting they're career and expertise in jeopardy by saying the things she said.

The engineer should of stayed humble, and expressed their lack of either understanding or knowledge, and taken ownership of the issue to stop boosting the frequency in question, instead of making up excuses like she did. A simple solution would have been riding the frequency; keeping your hand on the knob at all times and adjusting as needed.

You have to have skills as a monitor engineer to get the job in the first place so saying these things makes it look like you don't care and are a complete asshole. Besides it's the wrong things to say. We all know everyone makes mistakes and things like feedback happen, but there is a right way and a wrong way to go about it. Make an executive decision, cut the frequency and explain why later, or don't cut the frequency and explain why later, and do it knowing you're in the right. In other words explain what was going on in a humble way, but don't cop an attitude and start saying you don't know what you're doing, because as soon as you've said this you are done for.

Throughout all this Ms. Cook kept her cool the whole time, while the engineer went off the deep end at points, possibly being how she handles stress, and in the end seems to have a bigger ego than Ms. Cook did.

What differentiates egos and their perception to us? To try and answer, let's use the story above.

Let's be real here, of course Ms. Cook has a big ego, she's paid her dues and been in the game way to long to let anyone tell her she can't do this or that. She likes things the way she wants them, and if not, you will defiantly feel her wrath. However, most of the time when we hear the phrase big ego, we think of someone being a mean person, this could not be farther from the truth. Really, truth be told, mean people are mean and nice people are nice, and fame does not change this about a person, it only brings out their "true colors," so to speak.

Experience has taught me one thing: celebrities are normal people, really cool and quirky, and often misunderstood by people who don't understand the quirkiness. They can be jerks, sure, but the people who are not celebrities, and want to be, are the real jerks from my experiences.

Ever see a local band play at a local venue? Ever notice how they seem to be jerks, like they think they are gods and to good to talk to you, or very rude to people including their crew when they have reached some sort of fame in their hometown? If you have experienced this, chances are you put everyone in this category now; celebrities are jerks and think they are owed everything, or you walk away from the show bad mouthing the band and their big egos.

Almost seems bands, who gain a little bit of traction, think having big egos -the jerk attitude- and treating people like crap will maintain their reputation and coolness, making them sought after. The reality is these bands are bad people, without any respect, and are letting a little popularity go to their head.

Artists pick up attitudes from people on T.V., or people in the limelight, and therefore mimic them in hopes to get to the next level, without ever realizing, it's all a show put on for the cameras; they don't have the training to know when to turn it off and on for themselves. A little bit of fame makes them think people should do stuff for them and their attitude towards them reflects this by being a jerk because they don't yet get it. It's not that people shouldn't do stuff for them or treat them like gods, when they are gaining traction, it's that it shouldn't be expected and it should be a mutual relationship on both parties. The band should make everyone around them feel empowered, and in return, the people around them bring their life force and energy.

However, we can't say celebrities never have big egos, are never rude or way over the top; part of the quirkiness is the fact they are over the top in everything they do. The fact of the matter is, we are all human and we all make mistakes, and sometimes we have a bad day. No one is perfect all of the time. The difference is in how you react and treat people at the end of the day; snapping at someone, while not ok, does in fact happen to the best of us.

I am quirky in so many ways and have an over the top personality, but it does not necessarily translate into having a mean big ego. I expect everyone around me to strive beyond excellence and achieve the unthinkable, but I never expect what I am not willing to do. I am the first person to jump in and do or show, instead of tell. I never ask anything of anyone that I am not personally willing to do or have done before. If it's a new project and coming up with new, never been done, ideas is the mission, I push myself and everyone else to achieve and succeed, rather than expect.

Some people have told me I am too intense or over the top, and I secretly laugh to myself inside every time. Here's the rub, if you're saying this to me it means you don't have what it takes, simple as that. If trying to get you to stop smoking weed all day or right when you wake up, or trying to get you to exercise more, or to stop watching T.V. when you could be working on music is too intense, then you have shown me you are lazy and not cut out to make anything extraordinary out of your life.

Let's be real, if you're making $50,000 a year as a manager somewhere, or make more money than me, but wish you were making money with music like me, and I'm to "intense" for you, how are you ever going to make the transition out of your normal life?

The music industry is a tough road, no doubt about that, and we have to work extremely hard to get anywhere within it, it's just that facts. What separates the ordinary from the extraordinary is how we choose to live our lives. Actions speak louder then words, and motivation has to come from within. Life is way to short to be unhappy in it and I would much rather be happy doing what I love to do every day of my life, than sit around and complain about how unhappy I am. This is where our ego starts to shine through, the question becomes; Are you a nice or mean person?

Once we start striving for the unthinkable, people will start to get different impressions about us. These people will try and knock you down and say you will never make it, or explain why they are better than you because they make more money. They will use every excuse in the book to justify watching T.V. or playing video games on their day off while in the same breath, complaining about everything and getting upset by the littlest things. You know the type, they say things like "work sucks, I wish I could do what you do," or "I don't have time for anything, I work 50 hours a week (as they continue to play that video game for the 4th hour)," or "I'm so exhausted, work is killing me (even though every night they stay up until 1am playing video games or watching T.V. when they could of gone to bed at 10pm and gotten rest)." These people will look at us like we are crazy for choosing to work in music, because they don't realize they have become compliant in life, and seeing someone happy by doing what they want pisses them off.

We have to be careful once we stop being compliant in life and start striving towards our goals. People will misunderstand you and try to keep you on their level by not supporting you and continuing to drag you down with their antics. They will tell you your ego is getting way to big and you've changed.

People are perceived as having big egos once they've broken away from a mundane, compliant life, and start to become head strong, because they start to exude an authoritative aura that the mundane people can't comprehend. All of a sudden you're excelling at everything, or striving towards, and because you'd rather be working on a song, or wake up early to exercise, they think you're being a jerk when you try and motivate them to do the same.

For some of us, our attitude might change and we may become rude, or jerks by pushing ourselves to the extreme. Once we start to live a better lifestyle, the people around us who aren't doing these things could start to piss us off and our attitude towards them will reflect this perception. This happens because we start to see them in a new light, and look at them as being lazy or unmotivated in life.

The worse thing we can do is alienate our friends, and the people close to us, by looking down at them and treating them badly. Remember, not everyone is motivated to be extraordinary, and we shouldn't view them as a loser because of it, at least not to their face or behind their back. What we should do is use this as an extra motivational tool to keep pushing ourselves to the next level. For instance, if our friend wakes up everyday and the first thing they do is smoke weed, use it to motivate you not to smoke weed at all, because you see how it affects them and their life, or you say to yourself "what a loser." You don't have to start running your mouth about how they are destroying their lives, keep your thoughts to yourself, but use the driving anger inside you to push yourself even harder. By keeping your thoughts to yourself it helps save face in front of friends and maintain your friendship with each other.

If you do have to talk with them about an issue, or why you think they need to stop something, take the time to be in their shoes before you talk to them. You'll want to get an understanding of how they might react should you talk with them: think about how you would feel in the same situation. This will allow you to sculpt the right things to say, the right way.

Helping out a friend does not equal being a jerk and getting mad to their face about something, you have to learn constraint and self-control, otherwise they will call out your big ego and jerkiness.

The flip side of all of this is you may loose or get rid of friends during the process. I learned a long time ago I do not need people in my life that sit around and smoke weed all day long. Sure I have my long time friends that do this, and I would never stop being their friend, but I don't need any more people in my life like this, that's for sure. My friends who still do this kind of thing are a little more distant than they use to be because I need to stay motivated, and if they are not motivating me I don't need to be around them all the time.

I have most certainly let my ego get the better of me with some of my friends, not my better moments. It was a hard road for me during the initial phase of transition, I was always preaching how much better I was than them, and how they needed to change their life. Fortunately I was smart enough to realize how I was treating them before it got really bad and our friendship suffered.

I realized it was not them who needed change, but myself, and I needed to surround myself with smarter people who were motivated like me. Instead of preaching to my friends and hurt our relationship, it made more sense to stop hanging out with them so much, and in some cases that meant never seeing them again. If they are not on the same path, and bring you down, most likely they are not the right kind of friend for you. It is never easy to stop hanging around our friends, but looking at it like a career move helps.

Success breeds success; we need to surround ourselves around success. By surrounding ourselves around failure we are doomed to be a failure. Ego is therefore a result of striving to success and never looking back.

How your ego is judged is entirely up to you. Respect others and you will be respected. Treat others fairly and you will be treated fairly. Surround yourself around successful people and you will be successful. Keep your ego in check and everyone will become drawn towards you.

Confidentiality Agreement

Chapter 24

Everyone needs security.

✓ Full disclosure
✓ The agreement

We are all going to need some type of agreement at one point to make sure nobody steals our ideas, and to protect us from legal battles. Typically I will use what is called a confidentiality agreement when I am working with a new client for marketing and branding.

The basic premise for this agreement is to make sure they do not steal ideas from me once we start talking. A situation might happen where they agree to work with me for marketing or branding, but first they need some details about what I can do for them. For instance, they may request a copy of a marketing plan outline to assess if I know what I am talking about. Personally, I am all about giving people as much information they need to make the right decision for themselves, however, I also need to protect myself from them taking the information and never talking to me again. This is where the confidentiality agreement comes into play.

The agreement lets them know they cannot take my outline or ideas and sever our relationship while continuing to use said ideas and outlines. In other words, if they took my outline and ideas and stopped working with me I could sue them and collect damages from them if they continue to use my ideas.

Now this is an extreme example and the chances of this happening, in this way, are very slim. I am in no way a lawyer and cannot offer legal advice. I am simply explaining to you the reason for a confidentiality agreement and the purpose of using them. You should always consult your lawyer before you have any one sign anything or you write up an agreement. Legally speaking, I can only talk about and show you what one looks like for the purpose of education, again you should always consult a lawyer. This is not legal advice. Every state, and sometimes city, may or may not have specific rules and regulations for these types of agreements so make sure you do your research and talk to your lawyer.

Now that you understand this section is not legal advice and only a tool for education purposes, let's take a look at the confidentiality agreement I use.

Confidentiality Agreement

It is understood and agreed to that the below identified discloser of confidential information may provide certain information that is and must be kept confidential. To ensure the protection of such information, and to preserve any confidentiality necessary under patent and/or trade secret laws, it is agreed that

1. The Confidential Information to be disclosed can be described as and includes:

Invention description(s), technical and business information relating to proprietary ideas and inventions, ideas, patentable ideas, trade secrets, passwords, drawings and/or illustrations, books, patent searches, existing and/or contemplated products and services, research and development, production, costs, profit and margin information, finances and financial projections, customers, clients, marketing, and current or future business plans and models, regardless of whether such information is designated as "Confidential Information" at the time of its disclosure.

2. The Recipient agrees not to disclose the confidential information obtained from the discloser to anyone unless required to do so by law.

3. This Agreement states the entire agreement between the parties concerning the disclosure of Confidential Information. Any addition or modification to this Agreement must be made in writing and signed by the parties.

4. If any of the provisions of this Agreement are found to be unenforceable, the remainder shall be enforced as fully as possible and the unenforceable provision(s) shall be deemed modified to the limited extent required to permit enforcement of the Agreement as a whole.

5. All information (section 1) is to be released back to Discloser of this agreement at time of departure/ no longer working together.

6. Websites & passwords created for an artist by _____ will be given back to the artist in the unlikely case of the artist leaving _____.

WHEREFORE, the parties acknowledge that they have read and understand this Agreement and voluntarily accept the duties and obligations set forth herein.

Recipient of Confidential Information: *(This would be the person you're giving the information to)* Name (Print or Type):Signature:Date:

Discloser of Confidential Information: *(This would be you, the company giving the information to someone else)* Name (Print of Type):Signature:Date:

Empowering you Creativity

Chapter 25

The added value of this book

✓ Your homework
✓ My contact info
✓ 3 months extra support

You've completed reading the book! Congratulate yourself on taking the first step, and kick-starting your career. But the fun does not stop here; it's only getting started.

In this section of the book you will be asked some questions about what you have read, homework yes, and send them to me via e-mail. In doing so you will be signing up for three months of free, yes free, continued educational support.

My goal is truly helping you in your career, and simply reading a book, in my opinion, does not really lend the help and support you're going to need. So I have designed a program, for those of you reading this book, to help with applying the techniques in the book.

The Rules:

1. Answer the questions I pose in this section and e-mail them to me with the address provided.
2. Your three (3) months, free, continued educational support starts right away.
3. After three (3) months you will have an option to get continued support from me for a low monthly fee.

What's Included:

1. Google Hangouts with topics discussed in the book (bi-weekly).
2. Your documents reviewed and critiqued you've created using the techniques in this book (say you've just created your bio and need help knowing if it's effective or not, I got your back).
    a. This is only review, critique, and question answering. This is not an ask me to create a document for you (i.e.: I will not write your marketing plan, bio, pitch, etc.).

Your Homework - Sign Up for 3 Months -:

1. Send me your fact sheet (included real name and stage name)
2. Send me your 1 years goals
3. Ask me one question of you're liking, only one, in regards to this book
    a. Questions will be answered in Google Hangouts and/or via e-mail response back to you (I may not be able to answer directly to you due to high levels of responses, however, I am committed to doing my very best in answering everyone personally).
4. The best e-mail to use for answering your question and future questions you will have.

All questions must be sent to the address below when registering, failure to answer the questions in full will result in not being registered.

Send Information and Register: funksville@gmail.com

www.ingramcontent.com/pod-product-compliance
Lightning Source LLC
Chambersburg PA
CBHW080340170426
43194CB00014B/2638